How To PRAY For A Successful MARRIAGE

Volume I

Bill & Debra D. Jones

How To PRAY For A Successful MARRIAGE: Volume I

Copyright © 2018 Debra D. Jones LLC

Editing by Tamika Jones

All rights reserved. This book or any portion thereof may not be reproduced or used in any manner whatsoever without the express written permission of the publisher except for the use of brief quotations in a book review.

All Scripture references are from the public domain.

Printed in the United States of America

First Printing, 2018

ISBN: 978-0-9975563-3-9

Heartfelt thanks to Bishop P.E. Bryant, Sr. and Lady Yolanda H. Bryant, Drs. John and Evelyn Ogletree, and Elder J.P. and Missionary Novella Augustine for serving as our pastors, providing spiritual guidance and giving us examples of successful marriages.

CONTENTS

Foreword	vi
The 21st Night of September ~ Bill & Debra D. Jones	1
Man – Good Thing ~ Alice M. Baker	9
Love Deeply ~ Roosevelt & Gale Barden	15
Respecting Your Spouse ~ Eboni B. Barnes	19
ME TARZAN, you jane ~ Tammy M. Brackens	23
Marriage Marathon ~ Belinda Espy	27
Pray Without Ceasing ~ Minister Vivian J. Gipson	45
Let's Stay Together ~ Dr. Evelyn Ogletree	49
Help Mate ~ Rodney & Barbara Owens	53
Marriage Missteps ~ Gloria Riles-Walker	57
It Takes Three ~ Vernisha Shepard	63
Write The Vision ~ Elton & Danielle Simmons	67
A Marriage With Mirrors ~ Angela Scott-Torbor	71
Prayers For a Successful Marriage ~ Prayer Partners	79
Meet The Authors	149
Acknowledgments	179

FOREWORD

By Bill Jones

In the beginning, one of God's greatest gifts to mankind was companionship. He further strengthened this concept with the holy bonds of marriage. For two people to work at building a strong relationship over the years has to be heavenly blessed. Marriage is designed to last a lifetime, however in today's society that is not always the trend. Even with that being said, through the Help of God and His teachings through the Bible, He has shown us a path to loving Christian marriages.

Contained within this book is a collection of honest and personal chronicles the contributing authors are willing to share concerning their pathways to healthy and strong Christian marriages. These people have put in work, dealt with adversity, triumphs and controversy. They have experienced the ups and downs that occur within all marriages. They are willing to share what they have learned in an effort to be a blessing to others and please God.

It is my distinct pleasure to partner with my wife, Debra and the contributing authors and prayer partners in this book.

May God bless each of you.

INTRODUCTION

By Debra D. Jones

This book is what happens when God gives an assignment that is bigger than an individual. When God placed the idea in my heart, I was excited! I initially thought this book would be an anniversary gift to my husband, Bill. After all, I had written a best selling devotional – *How To PRAY When You Don't Have TIME: A Devotional* in 30 days and thought the task would be pretty straightforward. That was much further from the truth than I ever expected.

As I was preparing and God began to download information to me for the project, I realized if I wrote it alone I might be able to be a blessing to some people. However, if it was written with other authors and prayer partners, it could be a blessing to even more people. One of the benefits to the readers would be diverse experiences and perspectives that are relatable to many and have greater reach.

The first contributing author was to be my husband Bill, a brilliant man of few words. I was very encouraged that he was agreeable to participate in a project I initially thought would be a gift to him. Instead, our collaboration would serve as our obedience to God to share with the world.

I thought all the authors and prayer partners would be married, but again God showed me that some of the contributing authors would, in fact, have experienced marriage but are not currently married. We are honored by those that have been in broken marriages that are willing to be transparent to share their stories in the hope of preventing others from experiencing the same and providing healing for the pain that often accompanies divorce. Some of our prayer partners are single and share prayers for healthy marriages as well as prayers for future spouses.

I extended the invitation to the project and believed perhaps 10 or so would be willing to say yes. What I did not anticipate was more than 45 contributing authors and prayer partners lending their stories and prayers. The overwhelming response necessitated the books to be published in two volumes: *How To PRAY For A Successful MARRIAGE: Volume I & Volume II*.

The pages of these books contain tools to promote healthy marriages written by people from different cultural, ethnic, educational, vocational and socioeconomic backgrounds. The contributing authors and prayer partners are from all across the United States as far East as Pennsylvania and West to California. As you read our stories and prayers, you may laugh, cry and perhaps even have an 'aha' moment or two. Our hope and prayer is that you are blessed, and God is pleased.

How To PRAY For A Successful MARRIAGE: Volume I

The 21ˢᵗ Night of September

Bill & Debra D. Jones
Contributing Authors & Prayer Partners

One of the best days of my life turned out to be September 21, 1990. It was the day I met one of the most beautiful people God has allowed to enter my life. On that day and evening, it seemed a series of good fortune passed my way. Living in Houston, Texas all my life except for a few years away at college, I had experienced a lot of ups and downs that came with living in my beloved hometown. With the local 'Big Oil Bust' that lasted much of the 1980's, I was finally starting to regroup and get myself together. Life was now pretty good both economically and socially. I had recovered enough to have two jobs and a really nice apartment after years of having no job and living with my very caring sisters. I was coming up; I actually had a payday. It was all good.

On this particular Friday, a good friend, a buddy, my road dog suggested we hit The Strip, which was a collection of dance clubs on Houston's South Side. He suggested we start the evening by meeting at a new hot spot he heard of - *Club Savoy*. I agreed because I had money in my pocket and even a company car from one of my jobs. The club was in an area I was not familiar with, so I spent an hour trying to find it. Right as I was about to give up and go somewhere else, as luck would have it, I found *Club Savoy*.

I linked up with my friend at the club. After about two

hours, he said he was ready to go somewhere else. I said, "No, I'm not leaving. This place has everything, why leave?" He left and within a few minutes, the night went from lucky to magical. While sitting at the bar, checking out the crowd - there she was. I said to myself "That is a beautiful black girl." She was the most gorgeous woman in the room. In my eyes she was the most beautiful woman I had seen all night. Being a semi-shy person I had to devise a plan of action. I had to take a shot, a chance to meet her. I decided to take that long, long walk over to ask her to dance. Very direct, but it would be a very long and disappointing walk back if she said no. Magically she didn't say no, she got up out of her seat and led me to the dance floor. We danced to maybe four or five dance tracks. In those days, a person initially showed interest in another person by how long or how many times you danced with them. This was right up my alley! For a big guy, I had some nice moves and was confident in my dancing ability.

How can two people be in the exact same place and experience the same things but have entirely different recollections of the event? That is the case of our meeting one evening in Houston, Texas. We were both out dancing with friends. Bill asked me to dance and I recall declining because my feet were hurting from the high heels I was wearing, but extended an invitation to have him sit at the table with me and my friend Laureetha. Bill recalls it a bit differently – he said he asked me to dance and I ran onto the dance floor. Although that was decades ago and there is no agreement about whether we danced or not, we made an instant connection and are destined to live a lifetime as husband and wife.

The magic continued as I walked her back to her chair. I wasn't sure how I was going to continue our connection. She took all the pressure off me because she invited me to join her and her friend at their table. I was in seventh heaven. I was able to do things I was unable to do in prior years and had never done before. I offered to buy her and her friend drinks and she declined. Now she was after my own heart, not just looking to have someone to buy them drinks. I was now on cloud nine. This was unbelievable. A beautiful girl had danced five songs with me and now asked me to join her at her table. The same evening, an old high school teammate approached me at the club and said: "Bill, you don't want to mess with that girl, she's bad news." I said ok, but the entire time I was thinking, "She might want to mess with me and I will be around as long as she wants to see me." The rest, as they say, is history. Our bond has been strong ever since.

Bill accepted the invitation to sit at the table with me and my friend and we talked for a while. Our conversation was an easy conversation. It was obvious that he liked the lady that he asked to dance and I certainly liked the man that I was having an interesting, intelligent conversation with. It seemed like the time flew by and it was time for me and my friend to leave. I remember thinking he was taking his time asking for my phone number so I wrote 'Debra J' and my phone number on a piece of paper and slid it across the table to him and asked if he had a number. (It's hard for me to believe I was so bold, but I knew I wanted to talk to him again.) The rest of the conversation went something like this:

Bill: "I was getting ready to ask for your phone number!" (As he was writing his number down, he looked at the paper I scribbled my name and number on) "Your last name can't be

Jones."

Me: "Why not?"

Bill: "That's my last name."

Me: "Oh great, I won't have to change my name when we get married!"

Here's what happened next – he walked my friend and me to our car and we agreed to talk again in a couple of days because he would be working the next day and I had an event that I would be attending. We went on a date to a comedy show the following week and were inseparable from that day forward. I had met the man of my dreams, love of my life, best friend, priest of our home, and father to our son on the 21st day of September, 1990. We would marry on July 31, 1993. We celebrated 24 years of marriage July 31, 2017 but over the years one of us will send the other a message sometime on September 21st that says: "Do you remember the 21st night of September?" It is part of the lyrics to the song *September* that was sung by the 70's group Earth, Wind, and Fire. It is also the day that we agree that a match that was made in heaven was made known on earth.

Fast forward days, months and years later when I was in the den of our home on my knees praying for my husband. Well, I really was talking about him to God because I was mad at him for something he did or said that I didn't like. I can't even remember what it was now but I remember being pretty deep when I started praying and decided I would pray for him at least an hour. As I began to pour my complaint out to God, a strange thing happened: God began to speak back to me but it seemed like he was taking Bill's side. All I heard was what God was willing to do for me and He spoke it through my lips 'Create in me a clean heart and renew in me a right spirit. Make me a better wife who is able to help and be a blessing to my husband. Teach me Your ways, O' Lord....' Yep – it went on and on like that for a while. When I got off my knees that day, I knew God was more concerned about keeping our marriage healthy and our motives pure than He was about keeping score of who did what when and who was winning disagreements. If we are willing to go before God honestly and earnestly in prayer, He is willing to give us the answers we need to succeed.

We have a marriage that is perfected each day as we celebrate, laugh, cry, get angry, help each other, disagree, agree, get to know each other even better and share our lives. I am forever grateful for God allowing Mr. Jones as I like to call him, to find me and recognize that his good thing would love him, bring favor in his life, respect him, pray for and always want the best for him. In return, he has loved, cared for, prayed and provided for me in ways that I can never doubt are genuine and make me strive to always be the best wife for him.

The 21st of September will always be a really special day for me. A significant portion of my life began that day. Being naive to the way God works, I initially thought it was my lucky day. What I considered a lucky, then a magical day was, in reality, the day God had made. It was the day He decided to show me my soul mate. She is the person He said I would spend the rest of my life with and raise a family. That was the day God decided that it was time for me to meet the wife he knew was perfect for me.

Thank you Father for the 21st night of September and every year, month, day, hour, moment and nano-second that you have given us to share our love and marriage.

Therefore shall a man leave his father and his mother, and shall cleave unto his wife: they shall be one flesh.

Genesis 2:24 KJV

How To PRAY For A Successful MARRIAGE: Volume I

How To PRAY For A Successful MARRIAGE: Volume I

Man – Good Thing

Alice M. Baker
Contributing Author & Prayer Partner

He who finds a wife finds a good thing, and obtains favor from the LORD. Proverbs 19:22 NKJV

This is dedicated to the one I love, my husband, James Baker. I thank God for joining us together and continuing to make me your good thing.

Indulge me for a moment while I share a portion of our love story.

An elevator that services twenty-four floors of gainfully employed individuals, what a rare occasion to end up with one other person. I remember the day as though it just happened. I stepped into the elevator and cordially greeted in my usual manner and turned to face the door. The voice from behind says, "Why are you always so happy with a smile on your face?" I turned, looked him in the eyes and said, "It's because of Jesus!" He said, "He wished he had that." I told him he could and invited him to church. I shared that I could not sit with him because I sang in the choir and asked if he would be comfortable sitting by himself. He said he would, and I provided the pertinent information. Before I exited the elevator he said, "I would like to get to know you better" and my response was, "are you sure?" The man was intrigued by my response, and he was also a man of his word. He came to church that following Sunday and my pastor preached from Exodus 4:1-5, "What's in Your Hand?" He was captivated by the message and left looking at his hand.

As we began to spend time together, we grew fond of each other. After work one day, I planned to get my prescription filled for new eyeglasses, and he asked if he could come with me. When it was time to pay, he pulled out his credit card, and I was almost floored because I was a very independent woman. For the first time in my life, I experienced fine dining. Our first was my best; evening dinner on a riverboat seated by the window as the moon glazed upon the waters. Dining out was fine for him, but he will tell you that he fell in love when I invited him over for dinner and served smothered pork chops and cabbage. He also commented that he did not think he could live with me because I was too neat. I am sure he shakes his head sometimes now.

Well as time went on, he retired from the military and applied for a job with an oil company in Houston, TX. It made me feel sad, but I kept my feelings to myself. Later he shared he did not get the job. Imagine my sigh of relief because I was having the time of my life. Shortly after that, I received notice that my job is transferring to West Virginia. This was not the first time this topic of my job transferring occurred. In the past, my response was I could not leave my church. This time felt different because I sensed a tugging. I told the man I was spending time with that I needed to discuss something with him. When I shared that I had eighteen years of service and needed twelve and one-half years to retire, his response was, "Alice, this is not just a job we are talking about, it is a career, and you have to take the transfer." I was relieved and saddened at the same time. I questioned God, "Why would You send me someone who treats me the way I should be treated and then take me away from him?" I accepted the transferred and expressed to God, if this was my husband, He would have to move him to Winchester, VA. He drove my car up, and I was very sad to see him leave. We frequently talked on the phone the first couple of weeks, and then he told me he was coming for a visit. Of course, I was very excited, and that led to every other weekend. I left New Orleans in July, and when he came one weekend in October, he said he made that trip for one reason only, and that was to ask me to be his wife. I had already submitted my request to God, so there was nothing else left to do but accept his proposal. He took care of all the paperwork, and I flew down the week of Thanksgiving. The day after I arrived, I called my pastor, and we were married that day and have never looked back.

It was important that I share some of my history, so you will understand how significant it is to wait on God. Too often we make decisions without even consulting Him. As a matter of fact, we do the joining. Proverbs 3:5-6 says, "Trust in the Lord with all your heart, and lean not on your own understanding. In all your ways acknowledge Him, and He shall direct your paths." Too often we feel as though our sins will not be forgiven when 1 John 1:9 says, "If we confess our sins, He is faithful and just to forgive us our sins and to cleanse us from all unrighteousness." Too often we relax in low self-esteem when Psalms 139:14 tells us to praise Him for we are fearfully and wonderfully made; marvelous are His works....We must endeavor to reach the point where our souls know this very well. Weapons do form, but when we are in Him, they will not prosper. That which appears to be so dreadful is working together for our good. In times like these, I have learned to not fall for the bait of the enemy and ask, "What is the lesson in this for me? What am I to learn from this experience?"

Will there be challenging times in a marriage joined together by God? Of course, there will be many but, if we keep before us that we are always becoming one, there is no challenge that we cannot overcome. Also, remember that we are each individuals with strengths and weaknesses that complement each other.

We cannot allow the demise of a relationship to lead us to depreciate our self-worth. If you are that person, I challenge you to take your life back from the one who does not appreciate it and places it in the hand of the One who created you. He will love you as you have never been loved before. I am a living testimony that there is absolutely nothing too hard for God and at the appointed time, He will. When that man finds his good thing, there will be no issue with him loving and caring for your children as though they were his own. The favor that man obtains from the Lord will overflow into your marriage. The man who is sent by God is secure and not threatened when his good thing is called into ministry. My husband is very supportive of my calling, and I still respect him as the head of our household.

Do not miss opportunities that God places before you because He does have a sense of humor. I said I would never date anyone younger than me – my husband is exactly thirteen months younger. Before I knew his age, God revealed the godly qualities he possessed. This should be our number one standard. Too often we lower our standards for the sake of not being alone. In times of loneliness, we must draw near to Him, and He will draw near to us.

A couple of years after we were married, my husband shared he turned down the job with the oil company because he did not want to leave me in New Orleans. Now we reside in that very same state, happily ever after for 22 plus years. Teddy Pendergrass sang a song that says, It's so good lovin somebody. And somebody loves you back. To be loved and be loved in return. It's the only thing that my heart desires. Just appreciate the little… I thank God that we are not 50/50 nor are we each other's better half. We are 100/100. Since we are a unit, we are knitted together and gaining from each other's strengths and weaknesses.

I pray that the nuggets of our story will encourage someone not to give up or give in. Stay in the race, press your way through and see what the end will be. "But those who wait upon the Lord shall renew their strength; they shall mount up with wings like eagles, they shall run and not be weary, they shall walk and not faint." Isaiah 40:31

Waiting is our greatest struggle and our greatest asset. The benefits are well worth the wait!

…"Have you not read that He who made them at the beginning 'made them male and female,' and said, 'For this reason a man shall leave his father and mother and be joined to his wife, and the two shall become one flesh'? So then, they are no longer two but one flesh. Therefore what God has joined together, let not man separate." Matthew 19:4-6 NKJV

Love Deeply

Roosevelt & Gale Barden
Contributing Authors

Our Story…

October 16, 1982…..34 years, two months, 28 days, 14 hours, 27 minutes, and at this moment 42 seconds. That's the ticking clock on how long we have been married. It's more than half the years we've been living! God is truly AMAZING!!

What we knew coming into our marriage was that we absolutely loved each other beyond our very being. What we didn't know was how many ways and times this love would be tested! Tested to the depths of our finances, friends, family, our children, temptations, and trust.

Two scriptures sing out to me as we write our story. The first one 1 Peter 4:8 "Above all love each other deeply, because love covers over a multitude of sins" and Mark 10:9 "Therefore what God has joined together, let no one separate."

Covering a multitude of sins is what our deep love has done more times than we care to remember. We took our vows in a church in the presence of God. What I hold dear most about that day was how strong, and bold, and loud, and forceful my husband stated his vows to take me as his wife!

It was like he was shouting to the world that I belonged to him and that he was honored and proud to spend the rest of his life with me.

I recall me thinking that I could never match that volume or boldness. So, when my turn came to say my vows, I spoke in my volume softly, but sweetly from my heart with love, and we became one!

Throughout our marriage when the difficult and rough times come around, I often have to go all the way back to…..34 years, two months, 28 days, etc. and hear him saying his vows!! This along with amazing things that he has done during our marriage have demonstrated the depths of his love for me. It allows me to divert from the sin or situation or conflict that could lead to anxiety, more sin(s), separations, or even divorce. I can remember a very troubling time with one of our children and how my husband proceeded to shield me and comfort me even as his own heart was breaking. It's those moments that I draw on when we are in conflict as husband and wife or I have doubts about our marriage.

What God has joined together, let no one separate! For us, that is no one, or no one thing or things separate!

So how did we pray for a successful marriage, you ask?

I'm not sure that we ever prayed that exact prayer. What I know is that we prayed for our marriage individually, and together, and even at our monthly family prayer. Many times, just saying, "LORD HELP US!" Help us to forgive, trust, and understand each other. Let us stand in the depths of our love as we encounter good times and bad. Even in times when we feel we can't hold on to each other, let us hold on to

You God, and Your promise of what You have joined together, let no man put asunder. Just as You God showed the depth of Your love for us when You gave Your only begotten son Jesus, so that we could be reconciled with You and as a sacrifice for our sins, let us stay deeply in love so that we can be forgiving of each other and be in right standing with You. Thank You, God, for Your hands have always been on our marriage, and You have given us much grace and mercy. We honor You LORD and ask that You continue to bless us forever as time goes on…

34 years, two months, 28 days, 16 hours, 49 minutes, and at this moment 36 seconds!

This is our story and our prayer!

Respecting Your Spouse

Eboni B. Barnes
Contributing Author & Prayer Partner

Growing up as the youngest of three sisters I was regarded as the baby of the family and was treated as such. I was often told what to do, who I should and should not be friends with, which activities I enjoyed and how I should complete certain tasks. Even as I became a young adult, I continued to follow the pattern of doing what others told me to do. When I got married, my husband and I moved approximately 1,000 miles away from the people in my life that had primarily controlled how I thought and behaved. It was the first time in my life that I was free to choose what I wanted. I had a new last name, I was living in a new city and saw this as my opportunity to explore what I wanted and liked without fear of how my family would feel about my decisions. I was exploring new things about myself, and I needed the support of my husband to do so. Thankfully we had established early in our relationship a mutual respect for each other. One key element in establishing mutual respect is listening to each other and appreciating each other's unique personalities, ideologies, and idiosyncrasies. It's crucial to value each other's point of view. I recognize that often unintentionally we may violate this respect by insisting that our spouse see situations and/or circumstances as we see them. For example, your spouse tells you that they have always decorated for Christmas with an artificial tree and you express that your family has always had a live tree and you believe that it is stupid to have an artificial tree. By saying their way is stupid can be perceived that you do not value their point of view. This may cause your spouse to feel disrespected and possibly withdraw from you. It is of the utmost importance to acknowledge that there is no such thing as the theory of "it's not that big of a deal." If it is important to your spouse, you must make it important to you. Don't expect your spouse to read your mind. Express to your spouse if they have hurt you and be willing to hear how you may have hurt your spouse (Ephesians 5:21). By doing so, you demonstrate to your spouse that you are concerned with what concerns them. Empathy is a characteristic demonstrated by Jesus in his interaction with his disciples. He was concerned about the things that concerned them. Use this as your model for interacting with your spouse.

How To PRAY For A Successful MARRIAGE: Volume I

ME TARZAN, you jane

Tammy M. Brackens
Contributing Author & Prayer Partner

A relationship can face many challenges during its tenure. Individuals must make up their minds to stick to their commitment even when tough times appear. If a marriage last more than five years in this day and time, we are witnessing a miracle. There is no one antidote for the perfect marriage, but there are some techniques which can be implemented to help couples stay together. Some couples refuse to be cognizant of the fact that they are different and were raised in two different environments. Let's dissect the marital bliss or chaos of the fictitious characters Tarzan and Jane.

Tarzan and Jane, symbolize two different spectrums and ends of the totem pole of life. Tarzan is from the jungle. The jungle represents a world of disorder and chaos with barely enough to survive. He feels at home when things are out of order or when fussing and fighting occurs. Tarzan possesses an animalistic nature. He is wild and swings from tree to tree like a monkey. He is quick to act as opposed to thinking before he acts. After all, he is MAN: King of the human jungle without regards to the views of others BUT he loves Jane.

Jane is the polar opposite of Tarzan. Jane has been bred in civil society and has attended charm school. She possesses the best education money can buy. By the way, Jane lives indoors in a house. She was birth from the thought that ladies should be seen and not heard. Jane is poised and pristine and has rubbed shoulders with the upper echelon of society. Many good things have been invested in her. She has been geared to marry a man within her social circle. But, she has fallen in love with a man from the jungle named, TARZAN.

The marriage ceremony lends the two clients no manual on the perfect marriage, but each party makes promises before God and man to "fight for forever." "Fighting for forever" is a term I coined and gleaned from the marriage vows. The part that says, "Till death do us part" is the duty of each spouse to fight by any means necessary to stay together and fight to the finish. Each must fight temptations to leave, to cheat, to lie, to fall out of love, and fight urges not to love enough. If a burglar would unlawfully enter your house, you would fight to the finish for him not to prevail. With the same tenacity, each partner should fight to end the devil's reign in their families, lineage, and break the generational curses by refusing to separate themselves until death do them part. Marriages have ended over the silliest things such as cooking, money, friends and minor misunderstandings. Couples must not only point out their differences but appreciate them as well. Diversity has the ability to spice up a marriage. God has called the married couple to be ONE not UNDONE!

How To PRAY For A Successful MARRIAGE: Volume I

Marriage Marathon

Belinda Espy
Contributing Author & Prayer Partner

It's a beautiful day, and everything looks perfect. The bride is adorned in all loveliness, her groom is handsome and only has eyes for her. The pews are filled with loved ones and well-wishers. The Lord has truly blessed indeed.

Now, standing at the altar, the Pastor opens the Bible. It is at that moment; The Master is invited to attend.

"...Dearly beloved, we are gathered here in the SIGHT OF GOD and in the presence of this company, to unite this man and this woman in holy matrimony. Marriage was ordained by God and is declared to be honorable among all men. It is, therefore, not to be entered into unadvisedly or lightly – but reverently, soberly, and in the fear of God. It is fitting, therefore, that we should on this occasion begin by asking God's blessing upon this union. Let us pray..."

And pray we must...

HOLY MATRIMONY, REAL TALK

All things created by God and in the image and imagery of God reflects His Glory and His Majesty. Marriage is a miracle that can reflect God's Glory because it merges a man and a woman – the two becoming one, which usually means the merging of a household. Two people sharing the same space – which can be pretty tight quarters to be infused into, unless you have a plan. The best plan for a successful marriage should and needs to include God. It's no wonder that Jesus' first miracle was performed at a marriage reception (John 2: 1-11). He was invited and was not an intruder. Because He was invited, He was moved with compassion to save the dignity of the newlyweds when they ran out of wine. Jesus created a miraculous 'new wine' that was better than the old wine that had run out. What a great example of The Lord's love and concern for us in all areas of our lives. When we 'run out,' He can create something new. It takes His creative power to mature us to the level needed to dwell together in a loving and healthy marriage. He's always interested in creating 'new wine' that's better than the old. He loves to help us keep it 'fresh,' and in a marriage, freshness is vital. Submitting our marriage to God's keeping power will make it Holy unto Him.

"DIVORCE IS NOT AN OPTION…"

Recently, my husband Earl, went home to be with The Lord. Looking back over the years, I'm remembering something profound that he requested shortly after asking me to marry him. He said, "Let's decide right now that DIVORCE IS NOT AN OPTION." I agreed, and God proved that when two agree on anything in His Will, He'll make it happen. Our life together lasted 33 years, with the journey beginning at the altar in 1983. Was our life going to be without woes? No way, but we were in love, and eager to begin our new life together. He was beautiful in my eyes, and frankly, the words and the vows exchanged that day were nothing short of perfection. "What can go wrong now? Everything was going to be wonderful." However, it's the word 'everything' that can be deceiving. 'Everything' will not always be wonderful. Trials and tribulations in your marriage will come. Daily sometimes. But thanks be to God, who ALWAYS causes us to triumph in Christ (2 Corinthians 2:14), we can overcome any obstacle.

God is Truth. His Word states that the union between husband and wife was ordained, and meant to be honorable to all - which means leaving mother and father, children, in-laws, sisters and brothers, cousins and friends out of the marriage 'inner' circle. Within that circle, there is only room for God first, then husband and wife. Anything or anyone else is an intrusion of privacy! We are to 'leave and cleave' to one another. The word 'cleave' means 'to stick, adhere, cohere, to become closely attached, glued together, a growing together.' The last definition 'a growing together,' truly depicts the marriage journey of a man and his woman maturing as they cleave together in intimacy with The Lord, and each other. This is the foundation of a successful marriage. God first, then husband and wife!

Wouldn't it be wonderful if we didn't have to deal with all the bumps in the road ahead of us? Some of the 'potholes' we most certainly will encounter can disable our relationships and cause hurt and damage that can be tough to recover from. My mother-in-law, after disciplining my husband when he was a boy, used to say, "You might get better, but you'll never get well!" She was old, so she had some wisdom. The wisdom implied here is, recovery and healing are two separate processes. Recovery begins with a change of heart. Change your mind, and you can change your life. Healing begins with forgiveness. Again, if the 'inner circle' containing our mate exalts God first, then His Word will guide you into and through the rough places, you will ultimately face. You're going to have to recover from many issues. You're going to have to forgive many many times. It all starts with a change of mind!

As much as I don't like to acknowledge the devil and his dealings in our lives, I think it's only fitting to realize that he is our opponent; a cruel opposer whose primary focus is to stop and nullify the plans of God. Marriage is the plan of God. Stealing, killing, and destroying is in the plans of satan. So, there's the war. Be ready for the next battle, because it will come - manifesting through the busyness of our schedules, financial problems, insecurities, raising children, health issues, and many other ways. But, in Christ who strengthens us, we can do all things, and we have the victory (Philippians 4:13)! Couples contend for the victory! Yes, the devil is sneaky - BUT - there's always a remedy for the attack. Seek first the King, His love, and advice. Every evil force will bow low when The Master is invited in –divorce won't be an option.

RECOGNIZING AND CHERISHING THE TREASURE

Treasure: "Cherish, Hold Dear, Prize, Value Greatly…"
Honor: "Highly value something — to appreciate, cherish and recognize it as a priceless treasure…"

Matthew 6:21 says, "For where your treasure is, there your heart will be also." This verse suggests that your treasure is primarily a matter of the heart. So in marriage, it involves recognizing the beauty and worth of your relationship with your spouse and then doing something to put that recognition and appreciation into action. Action speaks louder than words. It's about dedication, heart, and soul, to build strong foundational qualities into your marriage relationship. But, it takes the two honoring each other. One person cannot continually show love and honor without reciprocation. 'Lop-sidedness' in giving and receiving love, respect, and honor can end up in burn-out. Our 'feelings' become depleted. A 'whatever' attitude is allowed to enter and from then on it is downhill. Don't let it get to this point. Start NOW by changing your mind about what's broken and begin immediately with efforts to rectify and reconcile your relationship with your mate.

Love and honor in marriage must flow from the designed order. We have to build according to the set pattern God has modeled for us. How else can we 'forsake all others and cleave to one another' if we don't put a value on our spouse as a priceless treasure which speaks, "apart from You God, my mate is the love of my life, and I honor them above all else in this world." All else includes the children (yes, there I said it..), your parents, the pastor, friends, and anyone else outside the sanctuary of the marriage circle.

Here's some wisdom gained by experience. The husband needs to honor his wife's position as his wife, his queen, loving and doing for her above everyone. In turn, the wife should receive her husband's love and attention, and honor his position as her husband by being the life-giver in the relationship.

TO THE HUSBAND...

Ephesians 5:25 says, "Husbands, love your wives as Christ loves the church, and gave Himself for it..." Now, men, that's a severe charge. Jesus died for the church. He gave everything. What will you commit to?

Communication

This we do know. Men are completely different than women. The way you think husbands, is usually far from the way a wife thinks. Men are usually interested in getting to the point, what's the bottom line, and keeping it simple. But what you have to realize husbands, is that women are geared towards giving details. We enjoy filling in the 'blanks,' and coming up with solutions! I admit we women can tend to talk too much, give too much information, and ask too many questions that you men don't have a ready answer for. Women enjoy conversation and making plans. This is how we roll. However, it may lead to us fussing about wanting you to be in control, but yet we won't let go of the wheel. You may not be enjoying the driving experience at all. This is a wedge that can be driven between husbands and wives. Unrealistic expectations. You expect something from her, and she doesn't get it – and she expects things from you, and you don't get it. The breakdown in communication begins, and you both begin retreating to your separate corners. Strife is in the house. Husbands, don't let this happen. How do you get your wife to stop all the talking and fussing and just listen to you? Assure her with tenderness that you hear her. The word here is tenderness; show affection. Be playful with her. Take the scowl off your face and the gruffness out of your voice. She will respond to your gentleness. State your case.

Ask her opinion. Compliment her answer. And, gentlemen here's a winner for you... Ask her to look in your eyes, and only when she does, ask her if she trusts you to pray about it. Then wait for her answer. If it's "yes," then there's your chance to get it right because Jesus will work with you, husband! But, make sure you pray!

Her Body
Husbands, there will be many issues to work through during the marriage journey with your wife. Because men are usually extremely visual, this is a 'biggy.' This is about body image and weight changes... (run for cover!). Getting to the point, please have an understanding that a woman's body can look and feel differently after having children and also as she ages. Where she may have been 38-24-38 before having the kids or before age 45, may now be unrealistic. Cut your wife some slack regarding weight gain, especially if she's given birth. Give her some time to breathe. This will be a perfect opportunity for you to show honor by demonstrating affection and speaking words of kindness to her. Even if she hasn't just given birth, but can stand to lose some weight, then show support. Be patient. You may say, "I've been patient, and she hasn't changed." Well, start by taking a good look at your own body. Do you look the same as you did when you met her? Are you fit and trim? What is she looking at when she sees you? If you can realize she may need your help instead of criticism, then come up with a plan that will benefit you both. Begin by suggesting the two of you start eating differently and working out together. Yes, you work out with her. This will encourage her to become interested in trying to look her best again. And guess what? If you compliment and coach her through the weight loss

process, she will want to please you in so many ways! Women thrive on sincere compliments. Otherwise, if you pull away from her, she may become wounded. Also, this can allow satan to present other doors of temptation, which is later mentioned. Body image and sex appeal are important, but it isn't the most important thing in a marriage. What's most important is working towards keeping friendship, fun, communication, and genuine affection alive and well every day.

TO THE WIFE...

Wives, we not only birth and nurture children, but we contain the 'cool glass of water' that can be poured on the 'thirsty ground' of the human heart. Your 'cool glass of water' for your husband may be a soft answer or cooking his favorite foods and serving him (yes that's right, serving him). It could be letting him know that you always have his back and that you're always there to listen. Not to always talk (because some of us don't know how to stop), but to listen. A husband needs to know that he can trust his wife with his heart. In NLT Proverbs 31:10-12, a question is asked. "Who can find a virtuous woman?" This question is letting us know that a virtuous (highly moral, ethical, pure) woman is hard to find.

> Who can find a virtuous and capable wife?
> She is more precious than rubies
> Her husband can trust her,
> And she will greatly enrich his life
> She brings him good, not harm,
> All the days of her life...

A virtuous wife is a treasure valued higher than rubies. She holds her husband's heart tenderly in her hands, and her motive in the marriage is to greatly enrich and make his life better because she's in it! Never speaking ruin or acting out in frustration and hostility, but bringing 'good' to the table, every day. Yes, every day. This is pleasing to God. To honor and do this for your spouse is actually honoring and obeying God. Wives you might be saying, "This is not what I do, I'm not made up that way..." Well, remember, if God says it in His Word, then it is possible for us to achieve! You are not of the world. The world says, "Divorce IS an option." If you're a woman of God, then you'll do everything within your power to do it as the Lord says. His way, then we can expect His results. It's a daily walk that always needs the help of The Holy Spirit. Without His help and apart from Him, we can do nothing (John 15:5)! The life-giving love we give out, that 'cool glass of water,' must be 'dipped and served' from our well of overflowing fellowship with the Lord.

Wives, we see in The Word concerning our role in the marriage, words and phrases like, "Subject to..."Ephesians 5:24, "Submit..." Col. 3:18, "Obedient..." Titus 2:5, "Subjection and Obey..." 1 Pet. 3:1. Ladies, we're called to SUBMIT and to LOVE our husband, as he submits, loves, and honors Christ. But how can we love them like that? To get an understanding of the biblical definition of LOVE.

Let's read 1 Corinthians 13: 4-8. "**LOVE** is patient, **LOVE** is kind, not envious, **LOVE** does not brag, it is not puffed up. It is not rude, it is not self-serving (uh-oh…), it is not easily angered or resentful. It is not glad about injustice, but rejoices in the truth. It bears all things, believes all things, and hopes all things. **LOVE** never ends." So sorry Tina Turner, but love has got **EVERYTHING** to do with it.

Pray and ask for the God kind of Love to reign in your marriage. Ask the Father to fill your heart with the Love He speaks of in the scriptures. Then, put it into practice.

I RATHER YOU WERE HOT!

Rev. 3:16 "So then because thou art lukewarm, and neither cold nor hot, I will spue thee out of My mouth."

Marriage can be a continual love feast if you know how to 'work' it. Here's a powerful observation. In the life of a Believer, what we need on earth comes when we make our request known in heaven first. "…On earth as it is in Heaven… (Matt. 6:10)". This is the first step if we lack anything. If we're bankrupt in the passion department, then yes, we should go to God, who IS Love and ask Him for help. Spend time talking to Him regarding how we feel and be willing to take the steps for Him to free us. Sometimes, we first need to confess to the Lord what our issue is, then ask to be washed in the Blood of the Lamb, in order for hurts and wounds of the soul to be healed. Then our genuine emotions can flow. Authentic love is passion.

Passion is a fiery energized emotion that flares up when you fan the flames of smoldering love. I'm not speaking of lust, but the passion that flows from a heart of love. Even Jesus Himself expresses His desire about the condition of love He receives from us in Revelation 3:16. He hated indifference…being neither hot nor cold. He'd rather we be HOT in our love toward Him, and not lukewarm. Offering lukewarm love to Him will get us spit out of His mouth! How about that? So HOT is better wouldn't you agree?

The accumulation of negative emotions received from the relentless 'swirl' of life can bring sabotage to a passionate love life. We can become resentful, irritable, and indifferent, which left unaddressed leads to toleration instead of passion. With this being said, there is a remedy to revive the listless heart. Go back to your First Love. His Name is Jesus Christ. He's waiting for you. We have everything to gain if we enter into a worshipful love affair with Jesus by exalting Him above all. He, in turn, will shower us in a flood of love and fire far better than any human being can give. Every encounter with Jesus enlarges our capacity to receive and release love back to others; love ignited with fire and energy!

In a marriage, if the smoldering embers of love have grown cold, more action is required on your behalf. Here are a few tips to start the ball rolling in awakening marriage passion:

Be spontaneous. Whisper flattery in your mate's ear. Tell them what you love most about them…compliments, compliments…

Surprise your mate with a 'knowing' wink, accompanied by a subtle smile that says, "There's more to come" (make sure there is)…

Give them an unexpected passionate kiss while you're looking and smelling the way he or she likes…

Choose a special time to hold hands and speak the love language that only you and your mate understand…

That's fanning the flames. From there, the fire will erupt if you follow through!

However, if you think you may still need a little more help to get started on reviving your passion, then take a lesson from our King Jesus, The Lover of our soul, who is the ultimate authority on passion and faithfulness. "Kiss the Son lest He be angry with you..." (Psalm 2:12) What part of that verse do we not understand? Jesus is affectionate and enjoys the worshipful words we whisper in His ear! "Lord, there's nobody like you..." "Jesus, You're so so wonderful..." "I bless You Lord with everything I have..." "I give You my heart and soul Lord..." "I'm hugging and embracing You with my worship right now..." "I can't get enough of You Lord; You are THE BEST!..." Then guess what? The Lord will return your affection, and your heart will explode with His love which is infused with Love from The Father, and The Spirit as well! Powerful. Pure. Holy. The kind of fulfilling love which melts into tangible passion that you then can direct to your mate and others. All because you dared to first engage in intimacy with The Lover of your soul!

Father, thank You that I can come boldly to Your Throne of grace. I need Your help, Father. I want a passionate heart. Draw my heart close to Jesus first. Let Your will for this be done on earth in me, as it is in heaven. Set my heart on fire for You, and then for my mate. Show me how to demonstrate passion and tenderness. Heal me from hindrances and hurts from the past. I love You Father. Thank You. In Jesus' Name. Amen.

HABITS

Hebrews 12:1 "Let us lay aside every weight, and the sin which doth so easily beset us, and let us run with patience the race that is set before us..."

Sometimes we don't get a close-up view of our spouse until we live with them. Quirky habits like; snoring, excessive talking or the opposite, and mood swings, can tend to 'work on our nerves.' These 'little foxes' will turn into major disasters if not dealt with in a positive manner from the beginning. The first thing is to realize that none of us is perfect. For instance, loud snoring may be something a person can't help unless some type of medical intervention takes place. So, be the one who (gently) offers to help in seeking out the intervention. Other 'little' habits may be annoying, but they can be broken if you don't put condemnation on top of it. Offer to help each other overcome bad behavior.

There are even more detrimental habits than these that should be shared and revealed before marriage. To jump in and name a few major ones: the inability to be faithful to God or each other, drug and pornography addictions, dishonesty, alcohol usage, anger, violence, or criminal records. It's best to disclose these to the person you're going to marry sooner rather than later. Later can be devastating and lead to divorce. Marriage counseling is a great option when issues arise that you cannot solve on your own. Pre-marital counseling is highly advised, but anywhere in the journey is always a good place to begin. Having a neutral party hear and evaluate both sides of the issues at hand and offering a solution (hopefully Godly) can save your marriage from ruin.

1 Peter 5:8 "Be sober, be vigilant; because your adversary the devil, as a roaring lion, walketh about, seeking whom he may devour…"

Father, I ask that You through the Holy Spirit reveal every hidden thing in my marriage. Holy Spirit, show me how to pray concerning the problems we've been facing. Thank You that You're here to help us and show us the way to recovery. In Jesus' Name. Amen.

Satan has many ways that he may 'devour' us. The key word here is, 'may,' which means to give permission. Again, God gives us a choice. Obedience to God leads to His blessings. Disobedience leads to the curse. "I call heaven and earth to record this day against you, that I have set before you life and death, blessing and cursing: therefore choose life, that both thou and thy seed may live" (Deut. 30:19). God is so good; He gives us the answer to the test. Ultimately what you choose affects your family "...that you and your seed may live" Choose wisely. It's not just about you.

In this modern world, technology has evolved into the ability to have a vast amount of information readily available to the seeker. This is a great thing, but it also has the potential to become a major distraction. We use technology as an awesome tool to elevate our learning potential, and to provide information and facts as needed. But, satan always has a contrary agenda to the provision of God. In the case of technology, he has exalted his title and influence as the 'prince of the power of the air' to manipulate and sabotage many a good person through excessive and inappropriate texting, selfies, phone usage, and computer usage. It has also caused many of us to have our heads in a "down" self-centered position, and instead of being 'tuned in,' we're 'tuned out.' The art of conversing with one another is quickly diminishing, and in a marriage can cause a serious breakdown in communication with our mate and others if not careful.

To go even deeper into this, let's discuss 1 John 2: 16. "For all that is in the world, the lust of the flesh, and the lust of the eyes, and the pride of life, is not of the Father, but is of the world." These are several things that The Father warns us to watch out for. It is a reminder of the scene in the Garden of Eden when the serpent threw Eve a curve, twisting God's instructions by saying, "surely God didn't say...?" As she pondered satan's pernicious dissertation, a sprout of disobedience began to grow in her heart, and her flesh nature spoke for the very first time saying, "Go ahead, eat it, it's ok..." And so she partook because of his wicked directive, not realizing the repercussions of her actions would separate her from her Great Father and Friend. It marred the image of our God-likeness for generations to come. With her choice came the unbalanced influence over husband, ultimately causing him to sin and fall from grace as well (yes ladies we can have that kind of power over our mate). Now they were a couple, man and wife estranged from The Father because of making the wrong choice which led to disobedience.

Jesus said, "The man that even looks at a woman inappropriately with lust in his heart, has already committed adultery with her" (Matt. 5:28). So what's to stop us that live in this world today when lust, homosexuality, and exaggerated body images are readily available with the click of a button? One look, one click on a website can very well separate and captivate you into an addictive spiral that you may need help escaping from.

Statistics show that pornography usage within the church has reached an all-time high. It has affected pastors, as well as men, women, teenagers, and children in the pews. Jesus also said, "If your eye offends you, pluck it out..." You may say, "But I didn't 'actually' commit adultery," or, "I'm not 'actually' with another person(s)." Whether or not you think of pornography as harmful, remember this...anything done in secret, God will sometimes reveal publicly. Does this mean that someone will get on a microphone and expose those things for everyone to hear? Maybe. But, more than likely it will be revealed in your affections and emotional responses toward your mate. Your blessings are at stake. Indulging in pornography invites strangers into your imagination, which ultimately can spill over into your marriage bed. The Bible states that the "marriage bed is to remain undefiled"

(Hebrews 13:4). It is, (as a friend of mine told me recently and I agree) the 'holy of holies' between a man and his wife. It is a life-giving and pleasurable 'place' given and smiled upon by The Father...for us to enjoy each other sexually.

If this ministers to you, and you've been entangled in pornography and want to stop, start by obeying the words of Jesus. Pluck your 'eye' out by turning off the computer or telephone, then get on your knees and confess it to The Lord. He's there waiting to pull you out and lead you to further deliverance!

A Godly marriage is beautiful and rewarding. Not only do you have the privilege to serve The Lord together, but you have the benefit of walking through life with your closest friend, your spouse. It can be the best experience you will ever have!

How To PRAY For A Successful MARRIAGE: Volume I

Pray Without Ceasing

Vivian J. Gipson
Contributing Author

When I think of praying for a successful marriage, I think about all the things you have to learn during the process.

For instance, if you are married to an unbeliever, you must pray for him/her to be saved but, not for selfish reasons but for their lives to be whole and complete for their sake.

Secondly, you have to pray that God will deliver you and your spouse from bitterness and strife and that the Lord will cause both of you to be helpful and not hurtful to each other. The Word of God says, "And if a house be divided against itself, that house cannot stand." (Mark 3:25) "Above all else, guard your heart, for everything you do flows from it." (Proverbs 4:23NIV)

You have to pray and practice never going to bed angry. "Be angry and do not sin, do not let the sun go down on your anger." (Ephesians 4:26ESV) Pray that God will allow you to see your husband/wife as He sees them.

We are instructed, "So from now on we regard no one from a worldly point of view. Though we once regarded Christ in this way, we do so no longer." (2 Corinthians 5:16 NIV)

Pray also that you and your spouse will not allow pride to keep you from apologizing to each other. Let go of your need always to be right and critical of everything. "Through insolence comes nothing but strife. But wisdom is with those who receive counsel." (Proverbs 13:10)

Let's Stay Together

Dr. Evelyn Ogletree
Contributing Author

My husband and I met in high school and married young at the age of 19 and 21. We both grew up in dysfunctional homes with parents of multiple divorces. This was the only model we had as our guide for what marriage was supposed to be. The word "Success" for us was not used in the same sentence with marriage. When we got married, I had never seen a successful marriage. My grandmother died at the age of 42 with a houseful of children. My grandfather never remarried, so maybe their marriage would have been successful, but it would not be a model I would consider following. My grandmother was uneducated, had thirteen children, cooked three meals a day, cleaned up after everyone, raised her children, and served her husband. Her joy was to go to church; making sure Sunday dinner was prepared first and going for a walk door to door to visit relatives up the road on Sunday evenings. She worked hard on the farm and had no voiced aspirations beyond her job as a homemaker. A successful marriage was to do whatever your husband told you to do and be grateful to have a roof over your head. My mother did not follow her mother's model either. She had dreams and believed in marrying quickly and divorcing him even quicker if she found out he was not the one. I learned from watching my mom that women should marry a man if he asked you to and if you could not stay with him, divorce him and keep trying other men until you get the right one.

My husband's parents were the same: both failures in marriage multiple times. Subconsciously, we were taught that a successful marriage was not possible and it was ok to get a divorce and shop around. We learned that we could try marriage out as many times as we needed to and if that person did not work, we could throw them back and try another one. No one taught us how to pray for a successful marriage. We did not know what qualities to look for or avoid when considering a marriage partner, nor were we given directions with our marriage license. So when we got married, we had no idea what we were doing, no premarital counseling or a successful praying couple to take us under their wings. We had no financial planning or budgeting classes, parenting classes, biblically based classes to equip us to be successful. Therefore, we were set up to fail. We went through our battles, immature and unprepared. We did not possess any weapons to build our marriage, but plenty of weapons to destroy our marriage. Every time we had an argument, "the divorce demons" were always waiting to lead us quickly down our personal path of self-destruction, division, and divorce.

One of the things our moms did right was to take us to church and make sure we accepted Christ as our personal Savior. At church, we developed a relationship with a powerful God. We spent most of our time in church, so when trouble came our way we knew how to pray and ask God for strength and direction. We grew up watching successful families on TV. They were our role models, our dreams. These "perfect" fictitious TV families did not pray or go to church. Our foundation was rooted in the church and believing God would make a way somehow! These families were perfect in our eyes, and it appears they did not need to pray or go to church. TV and church became my resources to build a successful marriage. Be careful to stay in church.

You need the church to balance out TV, the Internet, and media. As a little girl, watching TV and reading fairy tales, I made a determination not to get divorced, but to live happily ever after. How to accomplish this goal was unknown to my young husband and me. I held tight to my dreams, prayed, and learned day by day from my mistakes, hurts, and disappointments. We had many problems in our marriage, but it was our relationship with God and many prayers that helped us make 43 years of marriage. Together we learned so much! This is why we developed our marriage ministry! We want to help couples stay married, to train them, to teach them, to encourage them and share the keys we've obtained over these years; learning how to have a successful marriage.

The primary key is God! You must seek Him first, which means reading His Word, listening to the Holy Spirit for directions, obeying God; not the world and patiently waiting on God to mature us all. It was not easy staying together. It was a lot of sacrificing, forgiving, trusting God at His Word and waiting - patience and faith. He has been faithful to us. We are so happy we stayed together. Thanksgiving is family appreciation time in our family. When we all get together, I see the promises of God fulfilled on the smiling faces of my 11 grandchildren. It was worth all of the hard work and tears. A successful marriage is one that loves, lives, forgives and grows up together founded on the Word of God. Success is overcoming the mountains to finding and reaching your dreams. Keep going. Your success is just one mountain away. You can do it. You must do it. Your grandchildren are depending on you! Keep praying and enjoy the journey.

Help Mate

Rodney & Barbara Owens
Contributing Authors

Proverbs 31:10-12

Who can find a virtuous and capable wife? She's worth more than precious rubies. Her husband can trust her, and she can greatly enrich his life. She will not hinder him but help him all her life.

Two individuals coming together as one must have the same values and principals about marriage. My husband and I values and principals about marriage were entirely different. This was because I grew up in a religious family and he did not. So our views and ideas were different. My beliefs as a wife were demonstrated by my mother. She took care of the household responsibilities as well as the kids. I knew being submissive played a big role in the marriage and serving God. I was taught about being a helpmate to your husband and building him up to be successful. To never gossip to others about his shortcomings but take those things to God. To pray and ask God for all your needs. So, with these values and beliefs that I was taught that was the type of husband I wanted. On the other hand, my husband's belief system and values were totally different. He did not have anyone to teach him about what a husband was and how a husband is supposed to take care of his wife. So the information received was not spiritually or biblically based and was not God's blueprint for what a husband is supposed to become.

After joining in holy matrimony there was a division, and we were married, but we were not one as stated in God's word, "marriage should be two becoming one." Our marriage was in turmoil because it was not initially based on God's principles about marriage. It was still based on certain false beliefs such as being into self and always using the "I" statement. Money was being made but still spent on self. There was a lack of honesty, communication, trust, and betrayal. These are all ingredients for the enemy to use to destroy what God has put together. It was not until God intervened into our marriage and we began to study His Word and live according to His Word, that we began to understand the deadly sins that were destroying our marriage. So, with God's help, He began to restore and renew our marriage. By now my husband was becoming a new creature in Christ and began to follow God's plan

A healthy marriage must be anchored in God's word so that a clear role for the husband and wife is maintained. As you can see, what the devil intended to destroy, God saw fit to save. None of this was possible until we started living according to God's word and plan that He had for our marriage. Placing God first in the marriage, we began to see the fruit of our labor; love, peace, joy, and happiness. Now today, we can say our marriage has been tested, but with God's help, it stood the test of the enemy. This year we celebrate 25 years and counting.

How To PRAY For A Successful MARRIAGE: Volume I

Marriage Missteps

Gloria Riles-Walker
Contributing Author

The announcement of an upcoming marriage seems to trigger great joy, happiness, and anticipation. These feelings often carry over to the couple's family and friends as well. After which, a flurry of activity began in preparation for the wedding that does not end in some cases until after the ceremony has taken place.

Sadly, much emphasis is placed on planning the perfect wedding and little on God's plan for the union. "Thy word is a lamp unto my feet and a light unto my path." (Psalm 119:105 KJV) When clearly this should be the time to really pray and ask for God's guidance, instead, other things take center stage. The focus becomes one of finding the perfect venue, the most beautiful dress, the fanciest cake and the list goes on. This I found to be our first mistake and perhaps the biggest.

I have come to view marriage in four stages:

The Courtship

The Marriage

The Disintegration of the Marriage

The Forgiveness

The Courtship

"Call to me and I will answer you, and I will tell you great and mighty things, which you do not know." (Jeremiah 33:3 NIV)

The courtship was the perfect opportunity to explore what marriage really entailed and if we were ready to make a true and lasting commitment to each other. Instead, in our case, the courtship was based on physical attraction, sexual desire, and a desire to please each other. There were many red flags that were simply ignored and not addressed. There were occasions when honesty, truthfulness, and cheating were called into question and quickly dismissed. Instances that yelled for prayer and soul-searching were treated as bumps in the relationship that did not pose a serious threat to the success of the upcoming marriage. In other words, this wedding was going to happen!!!

The Marriage

"Except the Lord build the house, they labour in vain that build it: except the Lord keep the city, the watchman waketh but in vain." (Psalm 127:1 KJV)

It was foolish for us to think the marriage was going to survive knowing that from the very beginning we had so many unresolved issues. There were many occasions of "I'm sorry, let's start over," but a good foundation did not exist. It did not take long for the marriage to begin to crumble. The foundation was built on shaky ground held together by convenience and deceit.

The Disintegration of the Marriage

"Above all, love each other deeply, because love covers a multitude of sins." (I Peter 4:8 NIV)

Where there is no love, there is no marriage union; instead, you just have two people sharing a residence. In our situation, you had people that were linked by a piece of paper and not their hearts. When this happens unless both are willing to fall on their knees and call on Jesus the marriage is over. At this point, the marriage for me had become irreparable. It seemed that prayer itself was not working, but as always I found that God was there all the time.

The Forgiveness

"For if ye forgive men their trespasses, your heavenly Father will also forgive you:" (Matthew 6:14 KJV)

I could not believe that a person could be so callous and dishonest toward another person. Especially since wedding vows had been spoken, goals set and many obtained. Then I remembered a part of our wedding vows coming from Mark 10:9 KJV, "What therefore God hath joined together, let not man put asunder." Those words struck me like a bolt of lightning. I understood then what went wrong; God did not put us together, we put ourselves together. However, in all things, once God is in control there can be closure without hate. When God touched my heart, I realized that we shared the failure. Most importantly, I have learned to accept what God allows. The anger is gone, I harbor no ill will. I have asked God to order my steps as He guides me in all things.

How To PRAY For A Successful MARRIAGE: Volume I

It Takes Three

Vernisha Shepard
Contributing Author

One cannot be in a marriage alone. It is not a solo proposition. It is a covenant between two people, ordained by God.

I was married once. I had prayed for years that the Lord would let me meet and marry a man that loved Him and wanted to serve Him as much as I did. Eventually, that prayer was answered. I believed that one day this man and I would have a powerful ministry. Other than the Lord, we had many things in common. However, this relationship was not meant to last.

Our respective families accepted us immediately. His family said that I gave him stability. They were grateful that I had come into his life. My family said, "Finally, she thinks somebody is good enough." And my father, who was the most important person in my life, called him "My boy."

After years of having settled into domesticity, things began to change. That instability that the family mentioned began to show. He jumped from job to job, always looking for the bigger brass ring. Three years of inconsistency passed. Making important decisions about our lives without discussion or consultation with me, began to wear on me. We went to counseling. I prayed for him. I put blessed oil in his food; I even anointed his pillow with blessed oil. All of this unbeknownst to him, and I waited for the Lord to answer. Our pastor, who he seemed to greatly respect, counseled him alone. He would not listen. After five years of struggle and 13 years of marriage, our relationship ended.

I don't know what made my husband change. I am reminded of the scripture that speaks of Judas' betrayal of Jesus: "...And Satan entered him." (John 13:27). My husband did not become violent or overtly disrespectful, but anytime decisions are made without consulting your spouse, it remains disrespectful. And if there is disrespect, can there be love?

I still love my husband as a person. I harbor no anger or resentment. I know that relationships don't always last. Ecclesiastes 3 tells us that there is a time and a season to every purpose under heaven. Even though this covenant should have lasted for a lifetime, it was only for a season. Because I was, and continue to be faithful, God, in His permissive will, answered my prayer. For that, I will be eternally grateful. I pray that the next husband will be because of His perfect will.

I don't know if I will ever be married again (I believe I will). I enjoyed being married. I am the marrying kind. However, I DO know that I trust The Lord. I believe that the thoughts and plans that He has towards me are to give me a hope and future. And to those who read this, I say, don't give up. If you have gone or are going through a divorce, with consistent prayer and trust in the Lord, you too have a hope and a future.

Write The Vision

Elton & Danielle Simmons
Contributing Authors & Prayer Partners

Habakkuk 2:2 ESV

And the LORD answered me: "Write the vision; make it plain on tablets, so he may run who reads it.

Proverbs 29:18a KJV

Where there is no vision, the people perish

Matthew 6:33 ESV

But seek first the kingdom of God and his righteousness, and all these things will be added to you.

Proverbs 16:3 NIV

Commit to the LORD whatever you do, and he will establish your plans.

God placed in my heart at 17 years old to write down what I wanted in a spouse. Of course, my mind at 17 years old wasn't as mature as it could have been, but I made sure that I was specific in what I was asking for. I wanted him to first and foremost know and love God. He had to have a sense of humor, love and respect his mother (but not a mama's boy), etc. I ended up with around 150 items on that list. I prayed on it and tucked it away. Little did I know that I would meet my spouse my freshman year of college at 18 years old... I didn't know it at the time, but God had me praying for my husband that I would meet just one year later.

Getting married young, we had a lot of challenges. Communication was a big issue for us. We didn't have a problem talking to one another. It was the way we were talking to one another! Elton would bring up divorce, and I would act indifferent when that was the last thing either of us wanted. We were speaking death over our relationship and were not making any type of plans for our future. God got our attention. My wakeup call was through a dream where I was being so mean to my husband that I made him cry and he packed his things and was about to leave. Elton's revelation came after an argument. God showed him how his words felt from my perspective.

Once our eyes were opened to what we were doing to our marriage, we had to change things. Our communication with each other got better through prayer. We started praying together and reading the word and went to Barnes and Noble and bought a journal.

We started out writing our marriage goals (more date nights, more intimacy, better communication). Then we started writing down our individual goals and would pray for each other. We kept adding to the journal and noticed that a lot of what we had written down had already manifested. God was blessing us and our marriage. We were closer to God and to each other.

When we spend time in God's word and in prayer, God gives us revelation. When we get revelation from God, we write it down in our journal. We have a joint journal where we write the vision for our family. We also write down our prayer requests and the desires of our heart. Sometimes we fast and pray on the things that we write in our journal. We have learned to be specific in our prayers to God and have seen Him do miraculous things in our lives, and our loved ones lives. It's amazing to look back at what we've written not even a year ago and see how God has moved and fulfilled so many of our prayers.

We encourage all of our fellow married couples to start a journal together. Submitting your goals, dreams, hopes, and plans to the Lord ensures that His will be done in your lives and shows your trust in Him. It also helps bring you and your spouse closer together because your focus is on your future as one. It also opens up dialog about current issues you may be having and puts God in His rightful place as the one you go to for help. We can both testify that sometimes only God can change our mind and heart and put it back on track.

How To PRAY For A Successful MARRIAGE: Volume I

A Marriage With Mirrors

Angela Scott-Torbor
Contributing Author & Prayer Partner

Mirror, Mirror on the wall, please show me where our marriage did fall.

As little girls we grow up with the thought of marrying our knight in shining armor. Marriage was etched in our thoughts as being simply just like the fairy tales we grew up reading such as Sleeping Beauty and Cinderella. However, these were just fairy tales. In life you will have struggles in your relationship, you will experience the good, the bad and the ugly. But these experiences should come to make your marriage stronger. Therefore, examine yourself and see what you are doing to keep the home fire burning in your marriage.

Are you willing to fight to make your marriage work or are you willing to fight against each other to make sure that you destroy the marriage? It's strange how when you are dating a person and problems come up, you try to figure out ways to solve them but when you get married the enemy tries to provide you with an answer to dissolve the marriage. The truth of the matter is that the devil is lowdown and dirty, and he doesn't play fair. That's why it is important that we use the weapons God has provided for us in His Word.

"(For the weapons of our warfare are not carnal, but mighty

through God to the pulling down of strong holds;)" (2 Corinthians 10:4 KJV)

"For we wrestle not against flesh and blood, but against principalities, against powers, against the rulers of the darkness of this world, against spiritual wickedness in high places." (Ephesians 6:12 KJV)

So many times, in a relationship we look at our mates as the problem to the marriage falling or failing. Marriage is a joint venture. And from the words of a song we grew up with, it takes two baby. Also, we must acknowledge God in all things, for the relationship to work. It is all too important that we use the mirror of truth concerning ourselves to build our relationship to become its best. Examine yourself and be truthful to yourself, your spouse and God so that you become better in your relationship instead of bitter.

"Examine yourselves, whether ye be in the faith; prove your own selves. Know ye not your own selves, how that Jesus Christ is in you, except ye be reprobates?" (2 Corinthians 13:5 KJV)

Honestly, the vows taken in a marriage should be broken down and studied with a clear mirror or a clear mind before you say "I do," because more than often neither mate takes into consideration what they are really saying, "I do" to. It is so funny when we date each other we accept more excuses from each other, either blinded by lust or love. However, when we marry, we allow the enemy to convince us that we don't have to put up with excuses. Actually, these should have been the words we spoke before we said "I do" in the presence of God and whoever witnessed us saying "I do."

When looking in the mirror what do you see? Does the

mirror reveal brokenness, selfishness, a controlling spirit, a false sense of reasoning, or narcissistic behavior? Or, does it reveal a loving, kind, peaceful, gentle, open-hearted mate ready to give all of yourself to your mate?

> *"But the fruit of the spirit is love, joy, peace, longsuffering, gentleness, goodness, faith, meekness, temperance: against such there is no law. And they that are Christ's have crucified the flesh with the affections and lusts. If we live in the Spirit, let us also walk in the Spirit. Let us not be desirous of vain glory, provoking one another, envying one another." (Galatians 5:22-26 KJV)*

Since we have promised before God and man to love, to cherish and obey, in sickness and in health, till death do us part, let us fulfill this promise without stressing each other to the point of an unwarranted mental death while yet being physically alive. I am not in any way suggesting that anyone remain in a situation where their life is in danger. However don't allow the enemy to destroy a marriage that is salvageable through God's amazing grace. Take a good look in the mirror of life to see if you are guilty of causing death in your marriage. Began to speak life into a dead situation, evict the devil from your home if you have given him permission to take up residence.

> *"Having therefore these promises, dearly beloved, let us cleanse ourselves from all filthiness of the flesh and spirit, perfecting holiness in the fear of God." (2 Corinthians 7:1 KJV)*

You can absolutely find joy in knowing that God's Word has already spoken to the magnitude of how a wife is a good thing. As believers we should remember that God in His Almighty infinite power honors marriage and whatever is broken He is able to heal. So, it is important that we as wives know our worth in our marriage and realize that God has given us the power to build it up or tear it down. Take an honest step back and begin to take a good look in the mirror at what your reflection depicts, and ask God to give you what you need to build up your marriage and your home.

> *"Whoso findeth a wife findeth a good thing, and obtaineth favour of the Lord." (Proverbs 18:22 KJV)*

> *"Marriage is honourable in all, and the bed undefiled: but whoremongers and adulterers God will judge." (Hebrews 13:4 KJV)*

> *"Every wise woman buildeth her house: but the foolish plucketh it down with her hands." (Proverbs 14:1 KJV)*

God is the answer to all life problems no matter how the equation is set up. **GOD IS THE ANSWER TO ALL THINGS**. In all thy ways acknowledge the Lord and he will direct your path. (Proverbs 3:6 KJV) In your marriage and in every path that you take in life the answer lies in God.

I remember growing up hearing the words "People who live in glass houses should not throw stones." Neither the husband nor wife are perfect beings, and it takes the grace of God to perfect each of us to balance a loving God-fearing relationship.

> *"Jesus looked at them and said, "With man this is impossible, but with God all things are possible."" (Matthew 19:26 NIV)*

So many times, we start on journeys in life without consulting God. We have already mapped out what our future looks like, how many degrees we will master, along with what company we plan to retire from. Haphazardly, we also look for our future mate to be tall, dark and handsome or a brick house (36-24-36), chosen merely by their outer appearance or based on their annual salary. These things can quickly change which will only leave room for emptiness. Is this love or lust? Are we setting our eyes on the standards of the world instead of the standard of the Word? The bible says,

> *"But seek first his kingdom and his righteousness, and all these things will be given to you as well. Therefore do not worry about tomorrow, for tomorrow will worry about itself. Each day has enough trouble of its own." (Matthew 6:33-34 NIV)*

God's plans for our lives are so much more important than the minute imagery that we have planned for ourselves. It would be great if we could only see ourselves as God sees us. This would allow us to never put our will in place of God's will over our marriages or any place in our lives. God's ways are not our ways and His thoughts not our thoughts. He has the perfect plan for our marriages/relationships. We just need to invite Him in so we can see the blueprint that He has for our marriage. For He has the master plan and nothing could be better.

> *"For I know the plans I have for you," declares the Lord, "plans to prosper you and not to harm you, plans to give you hope and a future." (Jeremiah 29:11 NIV)*

In all actuality, the enemy comes in to kill, steal and destroy. He kills the sanctity of marriages. He destroys the relationship between husband and wife and he is ultimately trying to destroy the whole family.

Let's allow God's will to overtake our marriages. This will decrease the work of the enemy in marriages. Let us say yes to the will of God and no to what the world says is right.

> *"There is a way that appears to be right, but in the end it leads to death." (Proverbs 14:12 NIV)*

God honors marriage, and without really realizing it, we agree to commit to Him in our marriage. Most of us never consider the vows that we make to one another, on one of the most important days of our life. Without giving much thought to it, we say, "I promise to love, to honor, and obey, in sickness and in health, for better or for worse, until death do us part." Now that it has been days, weeks, months and years since you've spoken those words, you now think and say, "Wait a minute, I had no idea what I was saying yes to. I did not have a clue of the unseen future we were saying yes to."

There will be times in your marriage that you may develop some love/hate moments. My husband and I have found the key to our lasting relationship is that we never fell out of love for each other at the same time. God, along with growing up and maturing in the Lord, has allowed us to value each other for who we are and what we bring to the marriage. We were made for each other. I now know that my husband was created for me and I for him because we compliment each other and can recognize it now that we have evicted the devil from our marriage.

There are many areas that the enemy will come in and attempt to destroy your marriage. What will tempt you, may not tempt me and vice versa. However, there is a thing that the enemy knows will work against your marriage. So stay prayed up and fast as often as the Lord tells you. It is through the flesh that we get off track, so we must work on the thing that is required to kill the flesh. Whatever you like that is outside of your marriage, starve it and began to feed it with what the Word of God says. Know that you will have ups and downs in your marriage, but true marriage is wonderful if you will just allow yourself to enjoy the beauty of marriage.

> *"Being confident of this very thing, that he which hath begun a good work in you will perform it until the day of Jesus Christ:"* (Philippians 1:6 KJV)

It is my prayer that this will help someone's relationship in a positive way.

PRAYERS
For A Successful
MARRIAGE

Nia Abdullah
Prayer Partner

Dear Lord, make me a wife.

In my single stage, I understand that this is my time to build myself up. Proverbs 18:22 says, "He who finds a WIFE finds what is good and receives favor from the Lord." (NIV). This tells me that I must first be a wife first in order to be found. I am asking you to refine me into the woman you want for the man of God meant for me. Thank you for your favor and blessing. Allow me to be more like You. Allow me to be a help meet even in my single season. I pray that one day, my future husband will meet me and see You in me. This way he will know that our union is ordained by God. In Jesus name, I pray AMEN..

Vicki R. Alexander
Prayer Partner

Dear Heavenly Father God

I come to you on bended knees, thanking You Lord. Asking You Lord for your divine strength in showing Boaz who I am. Lord Father God, please allow him to find me where You have me at this time. Please, Lord, continue to mold and make me the woman that he is searching for that will be there to help him. Father God, You know all that is good and the purpose that you've created it. Please help me Lord gather oil for my lamp to be prepared. Please Lord let him have wisdom and knowledge of Proverbs 5. Let him practice the right way to do the right thing as I will practice also. Please Lord let this man be a man who wants to walk the way that pleases You. Lord bless the bond and union of the marriage I am praying for. Lord, I'm thanking you in advance for all the things you have done in Your Son Jesus' Name.
Amen.
Amen.
Amen.

How To PRAY For A Successful MARRIAGE: Volume I

Josephine Arthur
Prayer Partner

Dear Heavenly Most Gracious Father, I am coming humble, yet boldly before your throne casting all my cares upon you. God, I am coming before you lifting up marriages. I pray that you will have your will and your way throughout marriages. It's a union that you have put together. You honor marriages, now God, allow them to honor each other and remember the vows that we took before you. Bring back to their remembrance the love and kindness they once shared. Your word tells us love is patient; love is kind, it does not envy, it does not boast, it is not proud. It does not dishonor; it is not self-seeking, it is not easily angered, it keeps no record of wrongs. Love does not delight in evil but rejoices with truth. During the difficult times allow the husband and wife to call upon your name. Allow them to remember Agape love (which means unconditional love). If they will begin to just call upon the name of Jesus, You change the situation. You will soften the husband's heart. You will soften the wife's heart. Allow the husband to love his wife a Christ love the church. Allow the wife to be submissive to her husband. Your word tells us that anything we bind on earth will be bound in heaven. Anything we loose on earth will be loose in heaven. We bind up any spirit that is trying to come against marriages right now in the name of Jesus. We bind up any confusion or division right now in the name of Jesus. Lord open up the lines of communication between husbands and wives. We loose the fruit of the spirit over marriages right now in the name of Jesus. We loose love, we loose joy, we loose peace, we loose forbearance, we loose kindness, we loose goodness, we loose faithfulness, we loose faithfulness, we loose gentleness we loose self-control. Lord your word tells us anything we ask in Your Name it shall be done. Father, we are asking You to save marriages today, because we know love conquers all. We pray this prayer in Your Son Jesus Name.

Amen

Alice M. Baker
Contributing Author & Prayer Partner

Father, I pray for every woman who desires to become a good thing. Let my testimony be an encouragement to wait for that man to find them. In the meantime, let them pursue the thing you are leading them to without wavering. Let their ears be attuned to every instruction and respond in obedience. Thank You, Father, for all You continuously do for us. In Jesus' name! Amen!

Eboni B. Barnes
Contributing Author & Prayer Partner

Dear Lord, I thank you for the mutual respect that my spouse and I share. Although there are times in my day to day comings and goings, I may unintentionally violate respect of my spouse by imposing my opinions on him/her or by belittling his/her views. I thank You that my spouse and I are able to talk about what we need to restore the respect and trust between us. Make me speak gently and kindly to my spouse. In Jesus' name, Amen.

Vanessa Blaze
Prayer Partner

Heavenly Father, marriage is a blessing and the joy and companionship when two people find love with each other with a serving heart. Marriage is honorable and the husband and wife should always cleave to each other and commit in prayer for a sanctified union with the expectation of a lifelong partnership. I pray for anointed marriages that have God's blessings and are committed to each other for their lives. In Jesus name.
Amen

Tammy Brackens
Contributing Author & Prayer Partner

Lord, I pray for the couples who are struggling through the spirit of Tarzan and Jane years. Help them to appreciate the human being you created just for them. It is the trick of the enemy to find fault in the choice of God for our lives. Lord, help us to be grateful for what you have done in our miracle marriages. What God has joined together let no man put asunder (Mark 10:9). In Jesus Name! Amen.

How To PRAY For A Successful MARRIAGE: Volume I

Annette M. Burnam
Prayer Partner

When I was given this assignment, I thought I would sit down and just write a prayer out of what I had placed on my list to God. Pondering, trying to put it all together in my mind, I could not help going back to my first marriage, and what I would have done differently. I thought about whether I still had some of that same baggage I carried then; perhaps even the whole set, so I went to the bible as I try to do every time before I pray about something. I had always said in passing that I want to be married again. I have said I was waiting for my Boaz and I will be his Ruth. I said I wanted him to be tall, dark and handsome, have a great income, a home or even to purchase one that I would move in to. I also included on my list good health and good credit. However, now as I think about what makes a successful marriage and partner up with others to pray for successful marriages, I considered if my list made sense. Is it just a laundry list of physical and financial needs or does it go deeper than that? Sometimes the way God gets my attention cracks me up.

This is my Prayer for a Successful Marriage…

Most gracious Father, I come as humbly as I know how, with bowed head and spirit on bended knees coming to You to say thank you.

Thank you that I can come to You first and ask for forgiveness in anything I have done or said. Thank You for forgiving me even when I did not put You first. I come asking for forgiveness because as I approach You, God I don't want anything to hinder my prayers to You. I need these prayers to reach the supernatural realm; I don't want these prayers to linger on earth and not reach Your ears and Your heart. I come to You because you are Lord of lords and you are the God who created the heavens and the earth. God, I come praying for a successful marriage today. First I have to ask You to prepare me as a wife, a godly woman, someone who is sought after as a wife. Your Word says he who finds a wife finds a good thing, so God I ask to be placed in a position to be found. God, as your daughter, let me have a Psalm 37:4 heart. Let me Delight myself in the Lord because You said you would give me the desires of my heart. Let my heart line up with Your will. When my heart lines up with Your will, I will always hunger and thirst for You and put You first in all that I do. I will love You with my whole heart, mind, body, and soul. I will be the woman of God that you have created. Let me lack nothing in value; let my words be seasoned with salt, give me a forgiving heart. God if there is anything in me that will keep me from receiving Your best out of marriage, I ask that You remove it from me today. I know the plans You have for my husband and me; plans for our marriage to prosper. Continue to make any crooked paths in my life straight God as I present my body to you as a living sacrifice. I ask that You make my latter years better than my former. Keep me healthy, let no diseases come near my body. I ask Holy Spirit that my eyes will not grow dim and my hearing not only hear Your voice but, let me hear clearly. I pray my strength will be renewed. Let me eat the good of the land. In Mark 11:24, Jesus said, Therefore I tell you, whatever you ask for in prayer, believe that you have received it, and it will be yours. So, God, I am asking You to send my husband, send a godly man that puts You first, that has more of a hunger and thirst for You and Your word, send a hard-working man, a man to lead his family in a manner pleasing to You God. A man who would stand strong in declaring God's word and His promises over his wife and family. I pray that he would serve the Lord with his whole heart, that he has wisdom in finances. God let his steps be ordered by You. I pray that integrity and character be with him. God, I know that you are working everything out for both of us. I know that you are changing those things that are not of You that will keep us from receiving Your best. I trust in Your promises that this is Your plan for man and woman to be together in marriage; that it is Your design and Your plan. I thank You, Heavenly Father, for unions that You have joined together. I thank You that what You put together no - thing will separate or tear apart. I thank You that You are the third strand cord that ties marriages tightly together and they will not unravel. Keep Your hand on marriages through the bends and the curves, the narrow paths, the bumpy roads, roadblocks, and even times when the road is under construction. Keep us Father in your hands. Let Your face continue to shine on us. I know You have prepared us for such a time as this; to love one another, to help one another, to lean on one another, to pray for one another, and to fight for one another. When one of us is weak, the other will be their leaning post. Our prayer life will be so strong that when the enemy comes to kill, steal and destroy, we will recognize him and fight. We will stand in sorrow and sadness, good and happy times to be with each other until death do us part. God, I am thanking You in advance for this successful marriage. I thank you that You have given both of us the desires of our hearts. I thank You that You satisfy us with good things in this marriage. Your Word said that my husband would love me like Christ loves the church. I thank You. You said that my husband would be able to trust me to be a capable, virtuous woman and that the heart of my husband would be able to trust me so that he does not need spoil. Heavenly Father, I love You, and I thank You so much for loving us. I thank You that You have encamped your angels around our coming and our going; that You have covered our children and our children's children. Continue to make us wise to the enemy's traps and destructive ways, that we will not hear the voice of a stranger. Increase our faith, so we would have the faith to know that You are God. Fill us with wisdom so that we can excel as husband and wife. God, I thank You for that Your Word says Beloved, let us love one another, for love is from God; and everyone who loves is born of God and knows God. The one who does not love does not know God, for God is love. By this the love of God was manifested in us, that God has sent His only begotten Son into the world so that we might live through Him. In this is love, not that we loved God, but that He loved us and sent His Son to be the propitiation for our sins. Beloved, if God so loved us, we also ought to love one another. (1 John 4:7-11). I pray for all those searching for love of that perfect mate. They must first love You, the one true love that You give to all those who love You and know You and stand on Your Word and Your promises. So today you be glorified, You be the lifter up of our heads, you God lead, guide, and direct us so that as we go on this road that only the God kind of math can make one plus one to equal two becoming one. Thank You again for Your mighty awesomeness. Thank You for loving us so much that You gave Your one and only son. Today God, let us have a prayer life so we can pray about everything and worry about nothing. This is a journey that You have ordained, and again I say thank You, God. I love you so much, and there is nothing you can do about it. Loving my Christ.

Amen and bless God

How To PRAY For A Successful MARRIAGE: Volume I

Belinda Espy
Contributing Author & Prayer Partner

Father, thank You that I can come boldly to Your Throne of grace to find the help that we need in every situation. Thank You, Holy Spirit, because You are here to help me pray as I lift up (husband's/wife's name). I bless (husband's/wife's name) in Your Mighty Name. I pray for (husband's/wife's name) to be in health, wealth, and to prosper with abundant life in every area. Touch (husband's/wife's name) mind, soul, and body. Cover him/her in the Blood of Jesus Christ wherever he/she goes today. Lord, bless our marriage. Show us what Your desires are for us as a couple. Thank You for Your Love for us. I speak joy, love, and peace to our relationship today. Give me understanding and empathy regarding anything (husband's/wife's name) may be going through right now. Help me to be sensitive to his/her needs. I bless them according to Your Holy Word.

(Important: Ask the Holy Spirit what to specifically pray for concerning your mate right now. Then wait! When you 'hear' with the ears of your spirit, pray what you are hearing Him tell you...)

In Jesus' Name. Amen.

Felicia O. Hudson
Prayer Partner

Love Beyond The Veil

Psalm 42:1

As the deer pants for the streams of water, so my soul pants for you.

Father, Thank you. Thank you for choosing me to walk this path that will lead me to love you've chosen for my life.

Thank you for knowing…seeing…and still loving the imperfect me.

Comforting past pains, loosening their knots, removing their stain engraved in my soul.

For all the wrong choices, and accepting "love" that was not of You.

Psalm 3:3

But you, LORD, are the shield around me, my glory, The One who lifts my head high.

Thank You, God, for lifting my hung down head, opening my eyes, reopening my heart with Your sweet revelation "he's coming". You will send me the husband that will give me love the way I have given.

Teach me…show me…how to drown in Your word. Ready myself, steady myself….for You told me "he's' coming".

But I won't look for him Father, for I trust You.

Just like music from the earth, he's coming to love me back from the gradual decline wherein the sinkhole of lack I sit.

I'll wait….patiently.

I'm done knowing the glory and pain of "single".

I've let go so I can love. Not a comparison, but the genuine article.

Colossians 3:17

And whatever you do, whether in word or deed, do it all in the name of the Lord Jesus, giving thanks to God the Father through him.

So, I thank You God in advance for being able to pick my dress, make my lists, getting caught up in the who's and where's.

But NEVER forgetting to bow down to give You Glory, Honor, and Praise, for the Godly love we'll endure "Beyond the Veil".

Gisele Jolivette
Prayer Partner

God, Thank you for this precious gift of marriage.

Touch us in a mighty way as we walk together in unity. Holy Spirit, as we journey together as one, Keep us focused on each other as our marriage build with growth. Fill our hearts and mind with strength, patience, love, peace, kindness, respect and understanding. Lord keep our conversation free from anger and frustration, as we journey forward. Keep your hand upon us so that our light shine as the example of a strong, powerful couple. Keep us faithful to each other forever always as we journey on the path of your will. Shield our union from selfishness. Protect us from all attacks of the enemy. God, remain in the center of our marriage as we continually grow deeply in love together, and grant us wisdom to hear your voice. We glorify You, in Jesus name. Amen

Bill & Debra D. Jones
Contributing Authors & Prayer Partners

Heavenly Father, Oh how great You are and worthy of all praise, glory and adoration. We thank you for creating marriage and teaching us how to become one. We pray that our marriage exemplifies what you intended and that we continue to seek you for direction in all we do including our marriage. We thank you for directing us in our lives in a way that allowed us to cross paths at the precise time that you intended. Lord, keep your hand on us and show us more about each other and You. We vow to keep you in the center of our lives. We thank you for protecting our marriage and preserving our love. We pray your blessings for long life, good health and a prosperous union. We bless and honor You in the Matchless, Marvelous, Magnificent Name of Jesus! Amen.
Amen.
And Bless God!

Cheryl Jones
Contributing Author & Prayer Partner

Father, in the name of Jesus, thank You for the beautiful union of husbands and wives. The church is Your bride, and You treat her with honor, respect, and love. Help us to live together in marriage to honor You.

Katrina Jones
Prayer Partner

Father God, Thank you for forgiving me for my sins. Your word says that I am to forgive others so that I may be forgiven. Even if I never hear the words "I'm sorry", grant me peace in all situations where I may become offended, angry or bitter towards my spouse. Help me to stay focused on the unconditional love that you have for me and in turn show the same compassion towards others. As conflicts arise, bring back to my remembrance that no weapon formed against me shall prosper and that I have the victory in the spirit of unforgiveness. Give me the discipline to stay focused on the calling you have for my life. It is through the power of the Holy Spirit that I find freedom in forgiving myself and my spouse. Hallelujah! In Jesus name, Amen.

Mattie P. Jones
Prayer Partner

Lord, Thank you for creating the institution of marriage. You established marriage as a union between one man and one woman. Lord, this gift has provided love, strength, and support to many of Your people. Most of all Lord, I am thankful for Christ's union with His people, the Church. Whether we are given loving and lasting marriages or never marry, we can still have a binding, exclusive relationship with our Lord and Savior who provides for our every need. Amen

How To PRAY For A Successful MARRIAGE: Volume I

Michael E. Jones
Prayer Partner

Proverbs 19:14

"House and wealth are inherited from fathers, but a prudent wife is from the Lord."

Ever hear the saying behind every successful man is a great woman? Two heads are better than one? We all have a cap on what we can humanly do, say, or think.

Prudence is defined as care or wisdom in handling practical matters; exercising good judgment or common sense. Even the busiest, most independently driven individuals need a companion. Proverbs is reminding us that it is truly a blessing to have a rock and companion that can always provide good, sound counsel. Money and wealth are positive, but they are only two of many things in life that must be managed with sound judgment. It's always great to have a companion to help "run a tight ship".

"Heavenly Father, thank you for your abundant wisdom. Thank you for providing clear guidelines to major life decisions and reinforcing that You will lead us down the correct path as we acknowledge You in all ways, including whom we choose to spend the rest of our lives with. Thank You, Lord. Amen"

How To PRAY For A Successful MARRIAGE: Volume I

Falisa Lemon
Contributing Author and Prayer Partner

Father, In The Mighty Name of Jesus I Pray for Marriages; I Pray the Rich and Righteous Blood of Jesus to cover each Marriage that finds this prayer in their hands. I Pray where there are issues in the marriage, Father God You will arise, step in and take control over all issues in The Name of Jesus. I Pray the Holy Spirit will give supernatural wisdom and understanding to everyone who reads this prayer. I Pray for the lines of communication to be open now, In The Name of JESUS. I Pray that every lie the devil has told, and every stronghold, every agent he has brought against these marriages are BROKEN NOW IN THE MIGHTY NAME OF JESUS!!! I Pray for more LOVE, HONESTY, LOYALTY, RESPECT, PATIENCE, PEACE, and JOY that surpasses all understanding. Oh, my Father who art in heaven, hallowed be Your name. Your kingdom come, Your will be done, on earth as it is in heaven. Give us this day our daily bread, and forgive us our debts, as we also have forgiven our debtors. And lead us not into temptation, but deliver us from evil. In the Name of Jesus AMEN!!!

Wendolyn Jones
Prayer Partner

Father

I pray that he is a man after your own heart.

I pray that this man's ears are pressed to your lips for Wisdom and Knowledge.

I pray that he is a man of Truth, Integrity, and Character.

I pray that he walks in the Spirit.

I pray that he is a Leader of his home and has influence in his community and

I pray that he meditate on the Word of God both day and night.

I pray that he is a humble man full of compassion and mercy for others.

I pray that he is bold and courageous in all of his endeavors.

I pray that he is a Visionary with foresight and strategic in his plans.

I pray that he allows you to shine your light so that he may find me and obtain favor.

I pray that you are the foundation of our Marriage.

I pray that the purpose of our marriage will reflect your love for the church.

I pray that our marriage is filled with love and your divine purpose.

I pray for daily prayer and meditation within our marriage.

I pray that our marriage will be one of ministry and help.

I pray that my husband will only have a love for me and I him.

I pray that he will talk to the Queen in me as I talk to the King in him.

I pray that your Will is accomplished in and through our marriage.

In Jesus' name,

Let it be so,

Amen

How To PRAY For A Successful MARRIAGE: Volume I

How To PRAY For A Successful MARRIAGE: Volume I

Pamela Lindsey
Prayer Partner

Father, in the precious name of Jesus, we pray for marriages! Marriage/family was the first institution created by You and therefore was and is important. Father, You even created a bride for Yourself to show us how much You desired such a union. Father, You showed us how important relationship is when You took the time to walk with and nurture Adam and Eve; You showed us how important communication is in a relationship when You talked with Adam and Eve. You even demonstrated attributes and qualities of faithfulness, accountability, repentance, and forgiveness, covering one another. So Father, first of all, we want to thank you for the institution of marriage. We want to thank you as well as ask for your forgiveness for sometimes taking this precious gift from You for granted. Then, Father, we ask that You cover marriages right now in the name of Jesus. We pray a fresh wind to blow over and revive marriages right now. We pray that You breathe into them new life. We pray that the blinders of satan and the world would fall off, and we would look at marriages and see what You see. We pray that we no longer compare what marriage should look like by the world's standard but by the one and only standard that really matters… the One who created it and that's You, Father, Your standard. We thank You for knowing what we would need in marriage and for supplying that need. Father, give us the wherewithal to be good stewards over the marriage that You have entrusted us with, and we will be ever so careful to give You all the glory, the honor, and the praise… in the Matchless Name of Jesus, Amen!

How To PRAY For A Successful MARRIAGE: Volume I

Minister Terry Marshall
Prayer Partner

Jesus, I want to take time out to say thank you for allowing me to write this prayer. My prayer is God to help me to be successful in the kingdom of God. Also in my prayer time, I am asking God to direct my path in everything I do and be the man that God called me to. My prayer to God to keep me and sustain me in my life. One of my other prayers is when God bless me with a wife. I Am asking the father to show me how to be the best husband that I can be. Lord allow me to continue to submit to your ways and your will. I Am asking God to continue to shape me and mold me. The best prayer I can give a person is to wait on God and allow God to deliver you.

How To PRAY For A Successful MARRIAGE: Volume I

How To PRAY For A Successful MARRIAGE: Volume I

Sonia Meeks
Prayer Partner

Father I thank you for the gift of marriage. Thank you for showing me that marriage is ministry for to minister means to serve. Help me to love my spouse through your word and by your word. Show me how to speak life into him/her and encourage them. Help me not to take things so seriously and enjoy the gift of love and friendship. You have blessed me with my spouse to be an example in the earth, so that others can see the love you have for them manifested in flesh. I pray to always keep the lines of communication open so that Satan cannot slide his way into our relationship. You have made me a unique being; therefore, I have the ability and power to be creative in how I love my spouse. I will not be or think selfishly, but always seek to remember that my spouse is my ministry. I will love them, cover them, and provide them with a place a safety. In Jesus name~Amen

How To PRAY For A Successful MARRIAGE: Volume I

Torin Murray
Prayer Partner

Heavenly Father I would like to start by reverencing your name and saying thank you for being my comforter, my rock, my fortress, and the lover of my soul. Lord, I come to you in desperate need of your help. Lord, you said that if I delight myself in you that you would give me the desires of my heart. Farther you know my heart and know that I desire a wife. Although I desire a wife Lord, I am not yet ready. I lack virtue, character, and morals. Before I can lead and be the head of a household Lord teach me love, patience, humility, gentleness, kindness, and the qualities of a good husband. Lord teach me these things so when I obtain my jewel I would cherish her, know her worth, and can demonstrate true love. Because you first loved us. Lord teach me forgiveness. Teach me forgiveness so that I can free myself and move forward from my past hurts. Lord I don't want to be selfish and burden my spouse with my past. Lord free me and fortify me on my journey on finding a wife. In the name of Jesus. Amen

How To PRAY For A Successful MARRIAGE: Volume I

Jay Pleasant
Prayer Partner

When I received the invitation to participate in this book, I thought "Why me? I'm a single mother, and I've never been married." So I prayed "Why me, Lord? I know Minister Debra has to be crazy." Then I heard Him say "Pray what I have taught you." GOD reminded me as he always does, THIS IS NOT ABOUT ME...

Prayer for your children's marriage...

The prayer of the single mother who realized that she needed to repent and pray for the future of her teenage sons.

I remember making peanut butter and jelly sandwiches, jumping in the car, driving to Galveston, Texas and pulling out the Bible and reading Deuteronomy 4:9 to my sons.

I started by explaining to them that my sins were not their sins and we were breaking the curses and all bondage so that when they date they will set standards and they will always treat women the way they would want a man to treat me, and we prayed.

Father, you know my sins, Lord I come to you with my sons, the sons you blessed me with, the sons that will stop all bondage, Lord don't let my sins be their sins. Father, I surrender them to you. Lord guide them to be godly men, men that will be husbands of your standard who will guide their homes through your Word. Lord, I ask that you raise them up to be fathers who will have the wisdom to lead their children, children an inheritance. Lord, I trust you. I thank you for the generations of families that they will bring into the world, healthy families grounded in your Word. I praise you in advance, in Your Precious Name. Amen, Amen, Amen.

How To PRAY For A Successful MARRIAGE: Volume I

Elton & Danielle Simmons
Contributing Authors & Prayer Partners

Father God, Thank You for our marriage, a union You put together. We submit all of our dreams, plans, and goals to You, knowing that You will prosper them according to Your divine will. Help us to write the vision for our family and seek You first in all things. We love You, Lord.

In Jesus' Name, Amen.

Joy Tharpe
Prayer Partner

Father, thank You for this day! Thank You, Lord, for Your grace and mercy. Thank you Lord for the anointing You have given to Your people. Lord thank you for Your Holy Bible that blesses the lives of your people. God continue to bless Your people with the gifts that will magnify Your name. I thank You, Lord, for allowing Your angels into our lives, a Word that is destined to bring Your people together that can never be broken because it was created by You! Guide our steps dear Lord for Your purpose in marriages, in the direction You would have us to go. Lord let the words that are written in this book enlighten someone's life, to draw them closer to You, in Jesus name Amen!

How To PRAY For A Successful MARRIAGE: Volume I

Angela Scott-Torbor
Contributing Author & Prayer Partner

2 Chronicles 7:14

If my people, which are called by my name, shall humble themselves, and pray, and seek my face, and turn from their wicked ways; then will I hear from heaven, and will forgive their sin, and will heal their land.

Father God, in the Mighty Name of Jesus we come to You asking You to reveal to Your people how, when and where to humble themselves, and Father God allow Your people to see themselves, for we are flawed and in need of Your grace and Your mercy. Father God, increase our prayer life and decrease those things that hinder our spiritual connection with You and Your people. Father God, we come against the very presence of evil, we cast down every lying devil, we cancel his assignment on all God's people and the Holy union of marriage. Father God, create in us a clean heart and the right spirit. Father God, we need less of ourselves and more of You. Oh, Heavenly Father rain down on us with Your spiritual anointing, fill us with the Holy Ghost so that we will go out and be about the business of our Father. Father God, I ask that You destroy the yokes of bondage upon the lives of Your people, God, encourage us to seek Your face. But most importantly God, encourage Your people to turn from their wicked ways and turn to the ways of the Lord. Oh God of Abraham, Isaac, and Jacob we need You like never before, our land is sick and is hemorrhaging severely, God we need an Azusa revival, send Your Spirit down oh Lord. Lord, heal the land. God, heal the land in the name of Jesus. I pray for a healing deep down in the souls of Your people. Lord, We cry Loud. We want to do a good work and not come down. Build us up God so that we live to please You and only You. In the mighty matchless name of Jesus Christ. I pray for victory in the land among Your people. Lives are being changed; souls are being saved, marriages are being made whole. God, we look to You, our eyes are on You. Save the sin-sick souls. Keep us in the palm of Your hand, oh God. May we forever walk in Your will and Your way. Amen, Amen, Amen!!!!

Meet The Authors

Bill & Debra D. Jones

Bill loves family and football. A former restaurant owner, he is most content when he is serving others, whether with his amazing culinary skills or as an usher in the local church. His best friend and bride, Debra loves family and travel. She is a prayer warrior and author of *How to PRAY When You Don't Have TIME: A Devotional* and serves in the local church. They are proud parents of one son, Michael, and reside in Texas.

Connect with Bill and Debra @ www.DebraDJones.com

Alice M. Baker

I am elated to be a good thing, mother, grand and great-grandmother, minister, and counselor. **But, my greatest joy is being a child of God!** After two unsuccessful marriages, God **never** divorced me. Instead, He enrolled me in His class and taught me how to fervently seek His face in prayer, listen to His voice and instructions, then, wait. I learned how to love and appreciate who He created me to be. The Spirit of the Lord revealed how my self-esteem and sureness of who I am was depleting; in spite of the numerous times my dad told me that I could do anything I wanted to do and be whatever I wanted to be. I pray that you will glean from my testimony and allow that man to find his good thing in you.

Connect with Alice @ arose01@att.net

Roosevelt & Gale Barden

Roosevelt and Gale Barden live in Houston, Texas. They have been married for 35 years and are the proud parents of three adult children.

Eboni B. Barnes

Eboni is a wife, mother, sister & friend. She is the owner of Kinderdance Houston where she teaches dance to preschoolers. Eboni enjoys watching her son play football & watching her two daughters cheer. When she isn't with family Eboni enjoys dancing & performing in local dance shows.

Tammy M. Brackens

Tammy Brackens is an innovative leader of the 21st century. She is an evangelist, intercessor, wife, mother, grandmother, entrepreneur, author and a liaison for the poor in spirit and knowledge. God has gifted this missionary with several talents to aid the people of God and the world. She has championed causes for the senior population, women, and children. She is a volunteer teacher for new moms who are incarcerated, has held civic positions in the community and former spokeswoman for low-income housing issues in her city. She has a passion for ministry and seeing the broken-hearted mended through the Power of The Blood of JESUS CHRIST.

Connect with Tammy on Facebook @tammybr

Belinda Espy

Belinda Espy, a native of Los Angeles, California is the ordained Pastor of **The Master's Kitchen** food ministry, public speaker, and worship leader, with compassionate fire and end-time prophetic anointing emphasizing the times and seasons. Her specific gifting is used to encourage the Body of Christ how to identify and walk in their own God-Given purpose.

Belinda was married for 33 years and served as head worship leader and co-musician with her husband Earl for 28 years, until his passing. She continues to sow into the lives of individuals who are hurting, suffering, and in need of physical and spiritual aid. Her passion for Christ and His directive for His Body enables her to minister the gospel of His Love, which has changed and influenced many lives.

Connect with Belinda @ msbelespy@yahoo.com

Minister Vivian J. Gipson

Minister Vivian J. Gipson, a Chicago native, has been an ordained minister of the Gospel since 1995. Vivian has been the Church Administrator of the Life Center C.O.D for approximately 25 years where she also serves as a member of the Board of Directors.

She graduated from Chicago City Colleges Program at Dawson Skill Center in 1976 and also received her Associate Degree in EDC at Roosevelt University where she studied Early Childhood Education. She worked as an LPN for 30 years and as a Teacher Assistant for the Chicago Board of Education prior to her retirement in 2009.

Connect with Minister Vivian @ vgipson21@gmail.com

Dr. Evelyn Ogletree

Dr. Ogletree, Executive Pastor of First Metropolitan Church in Houston, Texas, is affectionately known as Lady O. She has always had a close relationship with the Lord and has a special anointing that is revealed through her personal life, in her ministry, and her spiritual gifts. Lady O received her Doctorate Degree from Texas A&M University in Urban Education. She is a former school teacher for HISD, KISD and Cy-Fair ISD.

She is Director of the Infant Development Center (IDC) and Christian Academy that provides guidance and day care for children ages six weeks to five years of age, as well as leads an after-school program that is open to the community.

Lady O preaches and teaches the Word of God, speaks at conferences on subjects such as Marriage and the Family, Child Rearing, and does consultations for Ministers' and Pastors' wives. She is the founder of the Annual Women's Conference, "Women at the Feet of Jesus." She has been the keynote speaker at women conferences throughout the U.S. and abroad in Kenya, Africa, and Brazil. She is the author of A Day With My Father: Choosing The Path To Forgive.

She is blessed to be married to her husband, Dr. John D. Ogletree for more than 40 years; has co-authored a book with him and serves in the church with him. They have four children, all married and eleven grandchildren. Her joy is spending time with God and her family.

Connect with Lady O @ www.firstmet.org

LadyO@firstmet.org

Rodney & Barbara Owens

Rodney and Barbara Owens are the Founder and Co-Founders of Pathway to Serenity. They began their Pathway in 1997, and since then they have worked in the field of residential substance abuse treatment and sober living community. Through that journey, they recognized that their passion and calling were the same - to help addicted men gain a stronger foundation and become the men they were called to be.

They received the vision for Pathway to Serenity in 2005, and it became a reality in 2009. They are excited about the challenge that is ahead of them to be positive role models and to demonstrate by their actions that men may be able to find their own Pathway to Serenity.

Rodney and Barbara celebrated their 26th wedding anniversary in February, 2018.

Connect with Rodney and Barbara @

www.pathwaytoserenity.org

Gloria Riles-Walker

As an avid and dedicated bible student, I cherish the time that I am able to spend in the study of God's word. It seems that no matter how often I read the same scripture new revelations occur. Often times these new discoveries are a source of renewed spiritual energy.

After over 40 years in the educational arena, I am now retired. Most of those years were spent as an academic and career and technology counselor. I hold a BA in History/Government, an M.Ed. in Guidance and Counseling and certification as a Licensed Professional Counselor in the State of Texas.

I feel God has placed a special anointing on my life to be of service to his people.

Connect with Gloria @ gloriariles@yahoo.com

Vernisha Shepard

Vernisha Shepard is a licensed psychotherapist practicing in Houston, Texas. She has been licensed for over 22 years. She received undergraduate and graduate degrees from Tuskegee Institute and Howard University, respectively.

Ms. Shepard has certifications in anger resolution therapy and eating disorders. She greatly enjoys her work with women and adolescents. She is a faithful member of Harvest Time Church, and enjoys reading, movies, museums and the theater in her spare time. She is also a diehard fan of the Chicago Cubs.

Connect with Vernisha @ vyshepar@bcm.edu or (832)822-3692

Elton & Danielle Simmons

Elton and Danielle Simmons have been married for 11 years and have 2 children (Camille, 5 and Noah, 4 months). They met their freshman year at Prairie View A&M University and were college sweethearts.

Elton and Danielle both work in the Health IT sector and reside in Houston, Texas.

Connect with Elton and Danielle @
daniellebush36@gmail.com

Angela Torbor-Scott

My name is Angela Scott-Torbor, I am a native of Louisiana who moved to Houston, Texas after the voice of the Lord spoke to me from the book of Ruth. I am a Christian, wife, mother, grandmother, and nurse by profession for over thirty years. I live my life daily with a grateful heart knowing that, without God, I could do nothing and without Him, I would absolutely fail.

I have used both my Christian service and my skills as a nurse to spread the good news of Jesus in ICU units, in Labor and Delivery units, in Psych Units, in New Born Nursery Units, Clinical Research, and Heart Transplant Units. I have spent more than half of my life working diligently in the medical field to always try to make a positive difference in the lives I touch. I love helping people and spending quality time with my family.

I am an advocate for children and the elderly; it is my passion to serve and help those in need. As the founder of the non-profit organization, NFACT- Nurses For A Cause To Help Others, the desire to serve and provide support, empower, and see others progress is being manifested. It is my prayer to one day start an organization to help those who are broken and captive to the tricks of their enemy.

Isaiah 61:1-3 (KJV) - The Spirit of the Lord GOD is upon me; because the LORD hath anointed me to preach good tidings unto the meek; he hath sent me to bind up the brokenhearted, to proclaim liberty to the captives, and the opening of the prison to them that are bound.

I pray that my writing will inspire and encourage many. I'm honored to be among such great writers. I pray that this is the beginning of many more in my near future.

Connect with Angela @ aangelann@gmail.com

ACKNOWLEDGMENTS

Heavenly Father, thank you for trusting me with another awesome assignment.

Dr. Jinneh Dyson, an amazing coach with vision and insight that provided the clarity and push to write my first published book and has served as the blueprint for the subsequent ones. I will always ThinkUP! because of you.
www.JinnehDyson.com

Ms. Desiree Lee of DLeeInspires, a creative genius, my publishing consultant and founder of Authors in Business. Thank you for helping me publish four books in less than two years, create opportunities out of challenges and taking me on book signing tours to places I never imagined. You Rock!
#NoAuthorLeftBehind
www.DLeeInspires.com

Alice M. Baker, my friend and mentor. Thank you for all the many behind the scene hours you spent meeting with me in person and via video meetings to make sure this project was done in an excellent fashion. You are an incredible encourager and your willingness to do whatever your hands find to do well is commendable.
I love you sista friend!

Thank you for allowing us to partner with you in prayer for successful marriages.
Contact us at www.DebraDJones.com to purchase these books in bulk for bookstores, workshops, conferences, and events.

Other books by Debra D. Jones available at www.DebraDJones.com and online retailers

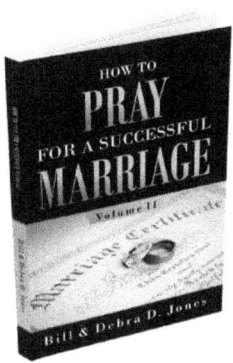

www.ingramcontent.com/pod-product-compliance
Lightning Source LLC
Chambersburg PA
CBHW051057160426
43193CB00010B/1221